THIRD MILLENNIUM MINISTRY

VOLUME ONE

Christian Life College
Faculty Project

CHRISTIAN LIFE COLLEGE PRESS
STOCKTON, CALIFORNIA

THIRD MILLENNIUM MINISTRY
Volume One
Christian Life College Faculty Project

✝

ISBN 0-9710411-6-4

Copyright © 2004 Christian Life College

All Rights Reserved. No part of this book may be reproduced in any form, except for the inclusion of brief quotations in a review or article, without written permission from the authors or publisher.

Unless otherwise noted Scriptural quotations are from the King James Version of the Holy Bible.

Published by:
Baughman Group Ministries and
Christian Life College Press
9023 West Lane, Stockton, CA. 95210
209.476.7840 - Email: info@clc.edu

Printed by:
Morris Publishing Co., Kearney, NE 68847
800.650.7888 - www.morrispublishing.com

Contents

	Foreword	*ix*
	Dr. Kenneth F. Haney, General Superintendent	
	United Pentecostal Church International	
	Introduction to the Project	*xi*
	Dr. Daniel L. Segraves, President	
	Christian Life College	

Chapter		Page
1	**Future Church**	1
	Meeting the Challenge of Changing Culture	
	Terry R. Baughman	
2	**From Fugue to Chorus**	35
	A brief history of the development of music ministry and the lessons that emerge from its study	
	Laura Payne	
3	**The Use of the Hebrew Scriptures in the New Testament**	53
	An Introduction to Canonical-Compositional Hermeneutics	
	Daniel L. Segraves	
4	**Everyone Needs Encouragement and Inspiration from Somewhere**	75
	Judy Segraves	

	The Grace of Inspiration	95
5	**Priceless Presents**	**97**
	Women's Ministries	
	Gayla M. Baughman	
6	**Involvement:**	**109**
	A Christian's Responsibility	
	Daryl Rash	
7	**Viability of Integrating Psychology**	**139**
	and Oneness Pentecostal Theology	
	Mark A. Segraves	
8	**Spiritual Disciplines**	**157**
	in a Postmodern Culture	
	Lonnie Vestal	
9	**Contemplative Prayer**	**171**
	Lectio Divina: Readings in the Classics	
	Robert H. Roam	
	Faculty Resources	*193*

To

Clyde J. Haney

who trained for the future

Acknowledgements

Simple tasks often turn into gigantic projects. Were it not for the capable assistance of several members of the staff at *Christian Life College* this faculty writing project would never have been accomplished. I gratefully acknowledge the contributions of the entire team at CLC!

First, let me recognize the tremendous contribution of literary scholarship. When I first proposed the idea of compiling a book of faculty writings, I suggested areas of expertise that each member possessed. They have exceeded my expectations. In some instances the contribution was in an area I did not know the author had studied or experienced. Heartfelt thanks to each contributor for pouring your efforts and abilities into this task.

All writers need the benefit of editorial assistance. Each chapter was reviewed and edited by at least three different readers. At every reading there were additional corrections suggested and typographical errors discovered. Thanks to the editing committee: Nancy Hunt, Gayla Baughman, and Lonnie Vestal for your valued service in producing the final project. A special acknowledgement goes to Nancy Hunt for her diligence in perfecting the articles and for formatting the pages for layout and design.

I sincerely appreciate the faith and vision which Dr. Kenneth F. Haney, former president, instilled in Christian Life College. The effects of that vision continue to guide us and inspire us to accept great challenges. Thanks are also extended to Brother Haney for the contribution of the *Foreword* for this volume.

Finally, I gratefully acknowledge the current president of Christian Life College, Dr. Daniel L. Segraves, who wholly supported us in this project with his words of encouragement, his own contribution of scholarship, a final editing with a keen eye for inconsistencies, and an *Introduction* to the project after a careful reading of each chapter (*including footnotes!*).

I trust this book will be a reference volume that you will treasure in your personal library for years to come. May it be the beginning of many future works as we study together the wondrous truths of God's Word and share them in print for others to read and enjoy.

Terry R. Baughman
Executive Vice-President
Christian Life College
Stockton, California

Foreword

We are living in momentous days. This is an awesome time for the church to arise to its full potential in ministry. We cannot miss our moment and fail at the task we have been given. This collection of writings addresses the concept of ministry in the new millennium.

Current faculty members of Christian Life College wrote the chapters of this book and each one will challenge you in some area of ministry. Regardless of your particular interest in ministry, you will find something that will help you in your pursuit of God and your desire to assist someone else.

My father, Clyde J. Haney, founded this college and his desire was to train laborers for the harvest field. He trained young men and women, not for his generation, but for future generations. After more than fifty years, Christian

Life College has alumni in many parts of the world living out my father's vision, reaching the world!

It has been my privilege to attend this college, to teach in it, to serve as its President and Chairman of the Board of Directors, and now to fill the role of honorary board member. I highly commend the fine work of the college and its faculty. I salute this wonderful effort, the publication of their first volume of writings by the faculty. I hope this will be an ongoing tradition, setting a standard of excellence in scholarship and writing.

Kenneth F. Haney
General Superintendent
United Pentecostal Church International
St. Louis, Missouri

Introduction

I am delighted to have some part in bringing to you the first volume in *Third Millennium Ministry*, a Christian Life College faculty project. It is our plan to release a new volume annually.

After reading each chapter, I am convinced that the contributions found here will be helpful to many and will have a significant influence for good in the 21st century Oneness Pentecostal movement. I found each chapter to be thoughtful, well-written, intriguing, and spiritually and mentally stimulating. The broad range of material will appeal to readers involved in a wide variety of ministries.

In the first chapter, Terry Baughman, who is planting a church in the East Bay area of Pleasanton, California, describes the fresh opportunities associated with establishing a new work in a culture very much unlike that of the early and mid-twentieth century American Bible Belt. You will find his treatment to be challenging; your creative impulse will be ignited.

In Chapter 2, Laura Payne traces the historical development of music ministry and offers significant insight into current trends. Her suggestions for further research are on-target, opening doors of exploration for scholarly research in the field of Oneness Pentecostal music. I think you will especially appreciate her call to integrate theology and musicology.

My contribution to the project is in the form of an introduction to canonical-compositional hermeneutics. I have long been fascinated by the use of the Old Testament in the New Testament, especially in view of the fact that of the hundreds of direct quotations and allusions found in the New Testament, over half are from the Septuagint, the Greek translation of the Hebrew Scriptures. My thesis that culminated the Master of Theology degree focused on this area of research. It is titled "An Application of Canonical-Compositional Hermeneutics to Psalms 14 and 53." Chapter 3 is a very brief treatment of this approach to interpreting Scripture. I plan to write more fully on this subject in the future.

In her usual delightful way, my wife contributed practical and inspiring help to all who have any interest in the writing ministry. In Chapter 4, Judy Segraves interspersed three of her stories to illustrate the application of her guidelines. Although I had read these stories before, I wept and laughed again. She is a gifted and published author, and you will find her chapter to be well-titled. It offers the encouragement and inspiration needed to motivate the writer in you.

I enjoyed Gayla Baughman's exploration of talents and gifts in Chapter 5. Before I read her contribution, I had never given much thought to the distinction between talents and gifts. In my mind, I suppose I lumped them together. But she makes a convincing case for a distinction, and her thoughtful counsel to a college student becomes an opportunity for all of us to expand our concepts of ministry.

Daryl Rash writes not only from a solid academic background, but also from a rich treasure of experience as a missionary in widely varying cultures. In Chapter 6, he discusses the responsibility of believers to achieve real integration in society while at the same time avoiding participation in those societal practices that conflict with Christian values. I believe he is right; only by means of such integration can we be salt and light.

I deeply appreciate my son's contribution to this project. Mark Segraves is a trained counselor who also possesses a significant theological foundation both on the undergraduate and graduate levels. His treatment in Chapter 7 of the history of thought as it relates to spirituality and psychology was enlightening, providing me with greater understanding of the issues involved with the integration of theology and psychology. His suggestions for further study provide clear and solid direction for future research. I am convinced that there is a desperate need for the ministry of Christian counseling, counseling that is rooted solidly in biblical truth and that grasps the complexities of human existence.

Lonnie Vestal's treatment of the value of the spiritual disciplines helped me better understand their contemporary importance. In Chapter 8, he explains how the disciplines contribute to spiritual wholeness. I have been somewhat frustrated for some time in trying to understand the Postmodern mind. Lonnie helped me to better grasp this slippery creature, pointing out both its dangers and its possible benefits for those involved in gospel proclamation.

I was inspired by Robert Roam's treatment of contemplative prayer in Chapter 9. I intend to integrate this practice into my own prayer life. I am a third generation Oneness Pentecostal with what is probably a rather typical approach to prayer and with minimal exposure to this approach to communion with God. After reading this chapter, I am convinced that it is possible to incorporate the Scriptures into prayer in a more meaningful way.

By the way, be sure to read the breathtaking poem on page 95! Terry Baughman, who wrote the poem, sent it to each member of our faculty hoping it would help motivate and inspire us to finish our contribution to this project. When I read it, I was awestruck and insisted that he include it with the volume. If you appreciate finely crafted literature, dancing words, and deep meaning, you will read this poem again and again.

I hope you enjoy reading this volume as much as we enjoyed bringing it to you.

Daniel L. Segraves, *President*
Christian Life College
Stockton, California

Chapter 1

Future Church
Meeting the Challenge of Changing Culture

By Terry R. Baughman

Terry R. Baughman, B.A., M.A.

An alumnus of *Western Apostolic Bible College*, Terry R. Baughman earned the Bachelor of Arts degree in Bible and Theology in 1977. He earned the Master of Arts degree in Exegetical Theology from *Western Seminary* in 1999 at the San Jose campus.

Baughman has served as an evangelist for nine years, an assistant pastor in Gladewater, Texas, and as pastor in the town of his birth, Canyon, Texas. The Baughmans planted a new church in Peoria, Arizona in 1989 and he served as pastor until coming to *Christian Life College* as College Pastor in 1994. He has served as the Dean of Students and the Academic Dean. In 2003 he was promoted to Executive Vice-President. The Baughmans are planting a church in Pleasanton, California – *The Pentecostals of Pleasanton* – and they are also active in the ministry of writing.

Future Church

By Terry R. Baughman

The chestnut mare stood three-legged at the hitching post completely at rest on a warm spring day. An occasional twitch of her ears and swish of her tail were the only perceptible movements as she shed the flies that had come to rest on her warm back in the late morning sun. Other than the occasional buzz of the flies around her ears, the only other sound was the call of a distant crow and the joyous song of the meadowlark in the nearby hayfield. That is, the only sound other than the steady drone of the minister inside the clapboard church house by which the mare was tethered.

The rhythmic rise and fall cadence of the preacher's voice had ceased to stir the mare or the other horses (and perhaps more than a few inside) who used this time for a nap in anticipation of the long trail back home after the service ended and lunch was shared on the grounds outside. It was a simple, predictable existence and weekly ritual, with only the weather and the success or failure of the crops as fodder for conversation among the men. The ladies busied themselves with preparations for meals while sharing the latest gossip about a budding romance in the community, or who just had a baby, or whether Aunt Velma's shingles might be contagious.

Less than a century ago *church* was very much a part of the lives of North Americans. Only the very pagan would miss church on Sunday and would likely be the subject of discussion during dinner. Church bells rang out religiously calling worshippers together in towns all across the land. Most states had laws regarding what businesses could operate on Sunday, and alcohol (where it was legal) was not allowed to be sold on *the Lord's Day*.

Entire communities were branded by religious affiliation: "It's a Catholic town" or "They are all Presbyterians." Communities developed a class system often based on the church you attended: "Oh, he's a Lutheran!" or "You know she's a Methodist," somehow implying their social acceptance or lack thereof. Social strata spread from the elite to the commoner then to the heathen, the unchurched minority in the community.

The Rise of Pentecostalism

Freedom of Religion was previously understood to be that one could join any Christian church of preference – Catholic *or* Protestant. Of marginal acceptance were the fringe groups, those perceived as later inventions, finding their roots in the brief history of American culture. The groups originating in America included Mormons, Adventists, Jehovah's Witnesses, and Pentecostals. From their fledgling beginnings and their tenacious grappling for acceptance, they have grown to be a dominant force in

Christianity. According to Paul K. Conkin in *American Originals*, "Today over half of all Christians in the world ... owe their conversion either directly or indirectly to the American missions efforts" of one of these groups.[1] Of the twenty-one million members in the United States, of these and other *American original* religious groups, "Pentecostals make up almost half of that total."[2]

Acceptance has not come easily to the *Pentecostals*. Often slandered as *holy-rollers* and social outcasts, they were commonly referred to as "the church across the tracks," a reference indicating they were on the wrong side of town, a society of the impoverished and underprivileged.

The last century has witnessed phenomenal growth in the Pentecostal movement. Life magazine, while ranking *"the top one hundred incredible discoveries, cataclysmic events, and magnificent moments of the past one thousand years,"* identified Pentecostalism as number sixty-eight. The report stated that, "today about a half billion people call themselves Pentecostal or Charismatic, and Pentecostals alone outnumber Anglicans, Baptists, Lutherans and Presbyterians combined."[3]

The phenomenal growth of Pentecostalism has been the source for much study among church growth specialists. One earlier study concerning the phenomenal growth of the Pentecostal movement in Latin America was entitled, *"Look Out! The Pentecostals are Coming,"* by C. Peter Wagner.[4] Wagner was appointed Professor of Church Growth at Fuller Seminary in 1971 and has been a leader in the church growth movement for more than thirty years.[5] What Wagner observed and predicted in the early seventies has been confirmed in more recent studies. Harvey Cox, professor of religion at Harvard University, stated in *Fire from Heaven*, "Several Latin American countries are now approaching Pentecostal majorities on a continent that had been dominated by Roman Catholicism for five centuries."[6]

Vinson Synan, Pentecostal historian and now Dean and Professor of Divinity at Regent University, Virginia Beach, VA observed in 1975,

> Pentecostalism seems now to constitute the wave of the future for Christianity. Some experts have predicted that after another generation or so, the majority of all the Christians in the world will probably be nonwhite, from the southern hemisphere, and *Pentecostal*.[7]

In his book, *The Century of the Holy Spirit*, Synan identifies the Pentecostal and Charismatic movement as "the most important religious movement of the entire twentieth century."[8] He continued in his assertion that,

> This movement, which now constitutes the second largest family of Christians in the world (after the Roman Catholic Church), is found in practically every nation and ethnic group in the world. By the end of the century, over 500,000,000 people were involved in this revival which continues its massive growth into the new millennium.[9]

If you were happy with the days when Pentecostals were unknown and uninvolved in the culture, you are not going to be very happy with the future. Pentecost has become mainstream. Some of the larger churches in America are now of some stripe of Pentecostal affiliation, and in civil government a member of the *Assemblies of God* serves as Attorney General of the United States.[10]

There are as many varieties of "Spirit-filled" Christians as there are of any other denomination, and the group frequently bends and blends the lines of denominational demarcation. You will frequently find "Spirit-filled" members among denominations that previously resisted, even demonized, those who demonstrated the experience of *glossolalia*.[11]

Pentecost is a rapidly growing movement that has not been easy to define or evaluate. About the time a new study is published and the numbers are neatly added, there is another outbreak of revival experience or another site of phenomenal demonstration and more books are written, studies have to be edited, the numbers increased, and growth patterns explained.

Pentecostalism isn't the only thing growing

While there has been tremendous growth among Pentecostal groups, there has also been expansion among various cults. In spite of the violence of the attack by radical Islamic terrorists on the World Trade Center, there has been an increased interest in the study of the religion of Islam. According to a website produced by the U.S. Department of State's *Bureau of International Information Programs*, "Islam is one of the fastest-growing religions in the United States today." A recent survey quoted on this website in support of this dynamic growth stated, "There are 1,209 mosques in America, well over half founded in the last 20 years."[12]

The Islamic community has expressed a radical agenda to change America from within by religious conversion. It should be noted that "between 17 and 30 percent of American Muslims are converts to the faith."[13] A direct quote from a fund raising letter by the South Bay Islamic Association (SBIA), which I have in my possession, was written to solicit funds for the promotion of the cause of Islam in America. It said, "As we strive to meet the demand for religious services from believers and would-be believers, we find ourselves straining for resources. We cannot, and must not stop, for we believe that it is our destiny to integrate the universal teachings of Islam into the every-day life of the American society."[14]

While mainline denominations are failing in recruitment efforts and suffering attrition in their membership, eastern religions and New Age cults continue to attract larger followings. Though they are called "*eastern religions*," the evidence suggests that they have migrated *west* in increasing numbers. The following statistics on some of these movements were recorded by John Naisbitt and Patricia Aburdene in *Megatrends 2000*:[15]

- There are 4 million followers of Islam in the U.S.
- The Moslem community in Colorado numbers more than 6,000.
- There are at least 600,000 U.S. Buddhists from the two main Japanese sects.
- There are between 3 and 5 million Buddhists of all varieties in North America.
- There are more than 40 Hindu temples and 500 Hindu religious organizations.
- In 1965 there were only 30 Korean churches in the United States; now there are 2,000.

Apostolic Pentecostals may think their mission is to convert the local community of Christians to the Pentecostal persuasion, when the truth is the community mission field has changed. Proselytizing must be changed to evangelizing. A whole new matrix of ministry must be embraced to reach our neighboring population.

America is *religious* but increasingly less *Christian*. The postmodern populace prides itself on reaching a new level of maturity by accepting all manner of religions and spirituality as equally valid. The downside of this pluralistic philosophy results in tolerance of any stated belief system—be it satanic, philosophical, or esoteric. There is no right or wrong, no good or bad, no true or false; everyone is right and nothing is wrong!

Freedom of religion is now more likely to be interpreted "freedom *from* religion."

The preaching of pluralism has taken root and religious tolerance has gripped the nation—except, that is, tolerance for evangelical Christianity! Efforts to silence the conservative Christian voice are strangling. The new American is open to all religions and closed to absolute truth, open to diversity and closed to moral values, open to civility and closed to Divine justice. *Freedom of religion* is now more likely to be interpreted "freedom *from* religion." *Christian America is rapidly becoming pagan U.S.A.!*

The present is only now

Changes abound. The horses and wagons and dusty trails of the last century have been replaced with automobiles, freeways, and speed. The demand for faster transportation makes airports as common as bus terminals. Communication with cell phones is more prevalent than with pen and paper. Today's generation of youth is more comfortable with computers and email than with an ink pen.

Community churches now attract congregants from miles away, especially in our metro areas. People are accustomed to commuting for work, for shopping, and for pleasure. So to drive ten, twenty, or even fifty miles to assemble with the congregation of their choice is no problem.

Church *and* culture are dynamic—always moving and always changing. About the time we get things defined, everything is different. We cannot find a hitching post to hang our hats on and park our buggies. If we do, we will be left in the dust of changing times. We cannot complain that "things aren't like they used to be" or "we've never done it that way." One songwriter said it like this, "One thing you can count on, things are gonna change."[16] Fortunately, we serve a God that is also dynamic, and He is up to the challenge of changing culture. It is "in him we *live* and *move* and have our being!"[17]

> **Church *and* culture are dynamic—always moving and always changing**

The Holy Spirit is uniquely described in terms of motion: rivers, the wind, and a dove.[18] It is significant that these are dynamic metaphors showing signs of movement, life, and change.

The powerful course of a river cuts a path wherever it wishes. It flows within its banks until the downpour of rain causes it to spill over, breaking out into new areas. Spiritually, floodwaters force us to relocate, to move from our lowlands of comfortable existence, and to settle in a new home on higher ground. That image evokes a powerful picture of the Spirit's work in the life of the believer, "Out of his heart shall flow rivers of living water" (John 7:38 NKJ).

The wind cannot be contained and maintain its identity. How can you house the wind? How can you box it, package it, and preserve it for some future day? Of course, it's impossible. Wind must be free to blow wherever it wishes and for as long or as hard as it desires. Jesus declared, "So is everyone who is born of the Spirit" (John 3:8 NKJ).

The dove is a gentle creature, cooing and fluttering about. But it is also living, active, and representative of the Holy Spirit. The image of a dove is a metaphor of peace and tranquility; its presence promises the comforting assurance that no danger is near. And so the Spirit moves into a world of chaos and brings order; He fills a life of turmoil and invades it with peace; His presence is that of a comforter who causes angst to disappear (John 14:16).

The Holy Spirit came with power on the Day of Pentecost, filling believers and creating a movement of epic proportions. The church came into existence with a dynamic display of phenomenal events: a mighty wind, tongues of fire, and speaking with other tongues. Peter proclaimed it to be the fulfillment of the prophecy of Joel, "In the last days ... I will pour out of my Spirit on all flesh" (Acts 2:17 NKJ).

This is the church, empowered by the Spirit; the church that Jesus said would be built upon the rock (Matthew 16:18). The metaphor of a rock brings to mind the image of solidity, steadfastness, and consistency – appropriate descriptions for the institution of the church – but this image does not lend itself to a movement of motion. However, the foundational cornerstone of this church is Jesus, and *He is a rock that moves!*

In the first Corinthian letter, Paul wrote of the example of Israel in the Wilderness. He spoke of the sea as being Israel's baptism. He referred to their spiritual food and spiritual drink of miraculous provisions. Then Paul said, "They drank of that spiritual Rock that followed them, and that Rock was Christ" (1 Corinthians 10:4 NKJ). This is not your normal rock! This rock *followed them* in the wilderness.

If we are to be a church founded on the rock, may it ever be the Rock of Christ, and may we move when He moves, and may we stand when He stands. Some movements have become institutions; their foundations became tradition and not the Rock of Christ. Some movements have become political; their foundation became material and not the passion of Christ. Other movements have become history; their foundation was sand. But the church must forever be a movement, founded on the dynamic Rock of Christ.

Erwin McManus, in his book *An Unstoppable Force: Daring to become the church God had in mind*, warned against losing the dynamics of a movement and the danger of turning our ministry into a monastery.

> So we turned our churches into monasteries—places that became spiritual havens for us, focusing on our spiritual life, caring for our spiritual needs, and nurturing our spiritual health.[19]

The church was never intended to be a monastery, a safe place and a sterile environment. The church should always be *a movement!* McManus wrote,

> When the church is a movement, it becomes a place of refuge for an unbelieving world. The church becomes the place where the seekers finally find the God they were searching for.[20]

We are part of a movement, the Pentecostal *movement.* Our heritage goes back to the Day of Pentecost ultimately, but initially, to the turn of the twentieth century, as the Holy Spirit was poured out on students of a Bible school in Topeka, Kansas, and on hungry seekers on Azusa Street in Los Angeles. We have a lot of history, a great heritage, and a glorious past. But, the *past* is no place to live! We learn from it and grow from it, but don't live in it!

To live in the past makes us irrelevant to the present and incapable in the future. The fastest way to become a monument of ancient glories is to park in the past and plan only for preservation. The pyramids of

Egypt stand in silent witness to those who sought only to preserve the present and failed to plan for the living future. Once the most powerful of kingdoms with a strong lineage of dynasties, the State is now the curator of the relics of a glorious past; it is now a museum, a monument to faded glories. The sphinx with the broken nose is an icon of a nation whose glory is *yesterday*, her best days behind, with little hope for a much different future.

Life is never static; it's always dynamic, ever changing. The present is only *now*, a thin ribbon of existence separating the past from our future. It is forever with us, snaking its path with ours; with each dynamic moment it moves the future into the past. So as you read this text (and as I write it), we are participants in movement; the future has become the past.

> **The present is only *now*, a thin ribbon of existence separating the past from our future.**

It's the same, only different

About the time we feel we have a handle on ministry and a grasp on the culture, everything changes. Like a sandcastle on the Pacific beach, the next large wave that surrounds the construction of painstaking care erodes the foundation, melts the walls, and flows back into the ocean. We can bemoan the condition of changing culture or we can jump on the train and confront the passengers with life-changing conviction.

Culture is at once changing and the same. Leonard Sweet in *Soul Tsunami* called it the double ring of postmodernism. He said, "One of the characteristics of postmodern culture is that opposite things happen at the same time without being contradictory."[21] It is like the toll of a church bell; the clapper strikes one side and then the other, but the opposite side rings the same bell.

Culture is at once changing and the same.

My grandfather, Mark Baughman (1912-2002), was an itinerant preacher for much of his ministry, preaching on the streets, under tents, in open-air meetings, in schoolhouses, and in numerous churches. He would strum the old *Epiphone* guitar and sing until a crowd gathered to hear his message. He was more comfortable baptizing in the creek than in a modern baptistery. After preaching the gospel message to any who gathered on the banks to watch and listen, he began to baptize the newly converted. Often someone would make the decision to be baptized right there on the bank and jump into the water, lining up with the other candidates.

It is different now, in that ministers seldom preach on the streets with only a guitar to accompany them. People are reluctant to stop and listen to a lone singer or preacher. Most of those who pass by are driving cars with windows rolled up (either because of fear *or* air conditioning) and are entertained with their own stereos.

Should we give up street evangelism? Not necessarily, but we need to adapt to the needs of our culture. One church group uses "encounter teams" on the streets to talk with people about their needs. Areas of need include drug/alcohol counseling, crisis programs for unwed pregnancies, and suicidal intervention, or countering depression. Leighton Ford, in *Christianity Today*, wrote about a young man who found a way to encounter gang members on the street effectively.

> You couldn't preach a sermon on the street corner to the guys ... because they wouldn't listen. But you could talk to them about their buddies who had been gunned down in the last year. You could ask how long they expected to live, then offer, "I am a preacher. Would you like me to preach your funeral? What would you like me to say?" From there you could tell them what you would like to have said at your funeral. What a creative way to communicate the gospel![22]

Now we seldom hear of open-air meetings, revival services in someone's yard or in a vacant lot. Can you imagine your neighbor's response? However, we might promote a "concert in the park" or get permission to host a gospel singing in a Wal-Mart parking lot, or set up an information booth at a fair or festival.

Tent revivals of a few decades ago have been replaced with camp meeting tents, coliseum crusades, rented auditoriums, and special events in the local church. The old one-room schoolhouse has now been replaced with a modern campus, and some churches utilize these modern schools to accommodate new church starts. Numerous small churches have morphed into larger churches with "small group meetings." Rather than using the schoolhouse, many churches now have their own expansive educational complexes.

Things have definitely changed, but have they really? We are still attempting, and hopefully accomplishing, the same thing, but often on a grander scale. We are attempting to reach more people, but there are more people to reach. We find ways to attract people to the gospel message and *we find that the gospel still works!*

What has changed?

Church is not viewed as much as a brand or an exclusive membership. Today's churchgoer is less likely to be "brand loyal," shunning all other church venues. Their membership in a local assembly would not preclude them from participating in other worship centers. Our "consumers" are accustomed to choosing from a variety of restaurants when they are hungry. Giant malls and shopping centers offer a variety of purchasing opportunities and a pocket full of multiple credit cards finance their adventure. Why would they view church as an exclusive (never look elsewhere) place of worship? Many don't, as they shop for benefits and convenience at their local outlets of religion. One offers educational childcare, another touts the benefits of a Christian school, while another promises contemporary music and shorter sermons. The choices are endless and become more diverse, from "drive-in" services to Christian clubs and hard rock worship.

Many newcomers are not accustomed to the concept of having a "home church." They are consumers—shoppers in the grand mall of life. When they come to church they are still looking for the best value, the freshest presentation, and the best youth program. They treat church like a spiritual smorgasbord, traveling down the line, picking and sampling, a little of this or that. Their kids may belong to a karate class at one church while enrolled in another's summer camp program. They may go to one church for Bible study and another for the live band and upbeat worship, while becoming a member in neither one.

> **When they come to church they are still looking for the best value, the freshest presentation, and the best youth program.**

There has been a tremendous shift in attendance away from mainline denominations, the neighborhood churches that were once the mainstay of every American community. Lyle Schaller in *Innovations in Ministry, Models for the 21st Century,* identified the following reasons for ministry organizational principles of the past becoming obsolete in current times.[23] I have added my brief comments:

1. *The erosion of denominational loyalties.* People are no longer interested in preserving denominational labels for identity. Have you noticed the proliferation of *non-denominational* churches?
2. *The popularity of the privately owned automobile.* People are willing to drive to a church where they feel their needs are being met. Frequently, members of a given congregation will pass dozens of churches to attend the one they have chosen. Gone is the premise of the *neighborhood* church.
3. *Public investment in excellent streets and highways.* This development contributes to the safety and ease of longer commutes. People now regularly commute daily distances that would have taken days to travel in a covered wagon.
4. *The change from a geographical to a non-geographical basis for meeting new friends.* No longer do you have to marry the girl next door or isolate your peer group to those in your geographical area. Travel, telephone, and now the Internet have reduced the size of the globe and brought the opportunity to communicate with anyone in the world into our living room.
5. *The emergence of a consumer-oriented society.* People become more selective in their purchases and more discriminating in their wishes. This has given rise to a whole new genre of churches—the seeker-sensitive variety. Their philosophy is to give the people what they want and require little in return.

6. *The sharp drop in the number of immigrants coming from Western Europe.* The majority of immigrants now come from very different religious traditions. The social mix has changed the look of our communities. The metaphor of a *mixing bowl* has often been used of our urban areas with the blending of cultures and ethnicity. A recent writer suggested it is time to update the metaphor from a *mixing bowl* to a *salad bowl;* each group of subcultures are part of the mix but they maintain their distinctive culture, language, traditions, and religion.
7. *The blurring of social class lines.* There is much more openness to blending in society and in the church. In many arenas social class distinctions have dissolved and there is more opportunity for interaction.
8. *The increased affluence of American people.* With affluence comes independence and the option of choice. People can afford to make some choices; when faced with the option, they may choose to go elsewhere *or to come to your church.*

The whole societal structure has changed and "family" is not the 60's family anymore. Many of us think of *family* as a mother, a father, and two or three kids, but today, if a family has two parents, it is probably a blended family. Due to the prevalence of divorce and remarriage (or even choosing not to marry) single parent families are on the increase. It is commonplace, or even "normal," for kids to have two or more homes as they rotate between parents and grandparents, spending the court-appointed amount of time at each place. Even singles that are in a "relationship" maintain their own homes ... just in case things don't work out. They may be "together" but live in separate houses and continue to live their separate lives.

> How can you have an attendance drive and press for perfect attendance when the kids are only with the "Christian" parent every other week?

As a result, even the simple question, "Where do you live?" may get a complex answer. How do you plan a visitation for your *Sunday School* class when you don't know which house they will be in this week? Or, how can you have an attendance drive and press for perfect attendance when the kids are only with the "Christian" parent every other week?

Other changes and challenges are more materialistic. The costs of land, materials, and construction have increased dramatically during the last few decades. Tremendous additional expenses challenge church planting in metro areas. Added to astronomical land prices, there are increased restrictions for land use, various developmental fees, special-use permits, and traffic or environmental impact studies. Planned communities have little use for tax-free parcels dedicated to building churches. All of these changes affect the planting of new churches and often discourage the missionary who feels drawn to the urban centers of America.

Aiming for the moon

The challenges don't become easier. Not only are we trying to find answers to the obstacles facing the church today, we must also engage the challenge to prepare for future ministry. It's not enough to find out where the church is in the context of our present world; we must also project where the world will be tomorrow and so prepare the church to be there to meet it.

One of the most profound illustrations of this fact was the manned exploration of the moon thirty-five years ago. The Houston command station prepared the flight pattern for the space travel of the Apollo and its three astronauts. It was understood that they could not target the moon, but rather they had to plot a course to where the moon would be when they arrived. How often have we aimed for the moon in our church efforts, only to find that it wasn't there when we reached for it?

How can we prepare for tomorrow? Schools, utility companies, and commercial enterprises must know the future! Why don't we? They must plan for future demand and determine population growth years before the fact. They conduct studies of demographics, check migration trends, analyze the job market, and study trends in the region in order to predict the future need for their products or services.

For more than twenty years a new community was meticulously planned in the California Bay Area, east of San Francisco on the eastern slopes of the Altamont. The community of Mountain House was planned to accommodate the migration of Bay Area residents out of the rising prices and congestion of the metropolitan area. In January 2003 the first foundation was poured for the Mountain House project, an entire planned community of 16,000 houses and a population of 43,500 people near the intersection of I-580 and I-205.[24] Before a street was paved or a foundation laid the planners could tell you where the houses and businesses would be built, where the schools and parks would be constructed, and whether or not the tax revenue would pay the bills!

While I am not suggesting that we plan our properties and our real estate acquisitions like that (if only we had those financial resources available), I am suggesting that we apply ourselves to the study of our community. Demographics of the city are often available to us from city developers, on the Internet, or through the Chamber of Commerce. Corporations spend thousands of dollars to study growth trends in order to prepare for the future of a community, all in the name of profits and commercial success. Why not take advantage of their studies to better understand our mission field? *Become a student of your community!*

Future-thinkers, future-preachers and future-leaders are needed if we are to be ready for the future when it arrives. We must embrace change and prepare ourselves for the viable ministry God has called us to. *Future leaders* are described by Samuel Chand and Cecil Murphy in *Futuring: Leading Your Church into Tomorrow*, as those who look at new paradigms of ministry, are future focused, embrace relevancy as a core issue, and are vision and purpose driven.[25]

The church is not The Church

Our emphasis should always be on people rather than properties, the person rather than the place. Often our goal in church planting is to "get a building," and the *church* becomes the structure. If we are to be successful in planting churches in metro areas, we must get back to this basic understanding: the *church* is the body of believers!

We are careful to quote the apostolic pattern in the *Book of Acts* in matters of doctrine, water baptism, and Spirit infilling. We are careful to avoid the traditions developed in the creeds of the early church. However, we have not been as careful to follow the *Book of Acts* pattern when it comes to the concept of church growth.

According to the apostolic pattern the early church had *no* buildings. As a matter of fact, it seems they were divesting themselves of all property and giving the proceeds to the work of the Lord (remember Ananias and Sapphira in Acts 5). Now, I am not suggesting that we teach property ownership as not biblical, only that we have mistakenly associated the structure as something spiritual. As soon as the Church was born they had 3,000 members, with 5,000 added in the few days following. There is no building program that could keep pace with that kind of growth!

It was noted that this growing, vibrant, New Testament church "went everywhere preaching the word" (Acts 8:4) and they met "publicly and from house to house" (Acts 20:20). They met in public meeting places, such as the synagogue. The synagogue of the New Testament era should not be thought of as a "church" but rather as a community center—a public meeting hall. The church is the church wherever it meets!

Michael L. Brown, in *Revolution in the Church*, maintained that we must change our thinking about the church to be consistent with the New Testament pattern. He said,

> In the first two centuries of this era, the Church experienced great growth without church buildings, and over the last fifty years it has experienced its greatest growth in countries such as Communist China, without church buildings.... Jesus is building His church without church buildings.[26]

Because of the long tradition of the Temple as a central part of Judaism, the original Christians, as Jews, might have assumed they too needed a Temple, a structure to unify this new group of believers in Christ. The New Testament record is conspicuously silent on any such effort or discussion of land acquisition or building of a worship center. Brown quotes Watchman Nee from *The Normal Christian Church Life,*

> Had Christianity required that places be set apart for the specific purpose of worshipping the Lord, the early apostles, with their Jewish background and natural tendencies, would have been ready enough to build them. The amazing thing is that, not only did they not put up special buildings, but they seem to have ignored the whole subject intentionally.... The temple of the New Testament is not a material edifice; it consists of living persons, all believers in the Lord. Because the New Testament temple is spiritual, the question of meeting places for believers, or places of worship, is one of minor importance.[27]

Consider the limitation of being restricted by the possession of property. In some instances, the majority of a congregation has moved from the area where the *church* is located. As a result, they either had to commute or change churches. Without ownership, it is easy to move where people live, relocating anytime it is needed!

Church growth is good. Crowded facilities and packed parking lots are exciting ... at least for a while. Then there is the pressure to build or to expand the facility. The focus and energy of the church is shifted from evangelism and continued growth to building projects and fundraising. In the mobile church environment, division and multiplication are easier. Small groups are encouraged as cell groups meet from "house to house" (again, *Book of Acts*) building up the community through fellowship.

Relevance in Ministry

In the future church we need ministries that meet needs, rather than fulfill traditional roles – real ministry in a fake world. The more artificial and veneered the world becomes, the more vital it is that the church be genuine.

> Rather than fighting technology, we must utilize the expertise for the benefit of church ministry.

With all the tricks and toys offered consumers, they expect a higher level of communication in the church, without the emptiness of entertainment. Our challenge is to provide relevant worship in a technological world, building community while embracing technology. Rather than fighting technology, we must utilize the expertise for the benefit of church ministry. Samuel Chand said, "We may not like certain innovations, but we can't get away from movement. If the past teaches us anything, it's that the methods we used a generation ago probably aren't effective now."[28]

Rather than expressing concern about people becoming obsessed with computers and isolated from human contact, instead see the technology as a whole new way of connecting with people. Try communicating with the church and potential contacts by email. Just last year Eli Lopez, youth pastor at Christian Life Center in Stockton, California, stated that 75% of his youth group used email to communicate! Utilize the Internet to spread the gospel and connect with believers.

I began to require an Internet assignment in a college class in 1998. The majority of the students did not know how to do a simple search online. So the first year I had to lug in a desktop computer, string a phone wire from the adjoining office, dial up the online service, and demonstrate how to do a search with the display projected on the screen with a 25-pound computer projector. Within two years I no longer had to demonstrate how to do a search but found that the majority of the class had a much greater understanding of computers and increased knowledge of their use. Now a 5-pound laptop has replaced the cumbersome desktop, and a high-speed Internet connection is available in the classroom to simply plug in through the Ethernet port. The mammoth projector has been replaced with a small portable LCD projector weighing less than five pounds ... and students can hook it up and show me how it works!

Incredible changes are taking place and the public is rapidly accepting this new technology. In a two-year period the Internet was embraced by more than half of the households in America. The following chart from data in the 2000 census shows a comparison of how long it took for 60 percent of households to adopt these various media technologies:[29]

1.	Telephone	30 years
2.	Radio	10 years
3.	Television	5 years
4.	Cable TV	27 years
5.	VCRs	10 years
6.	Computers	15 years
7.	Internet	2 years

We must use the technology available to us today! There is a *virtual* harvest field awaiting us as near as the computer and Internet service. In the year 2000, 45 percent of children under age 18 were connected to the Internet – more than 30 million children!

We are on the crest of a huge wave in youth ministry. Statistics show another boom in youth population similar to the "baby boomer" generation. Forty percent of the world population is under the age of 19.

At the same time, we are experiencing the "graying of America." With the baby boomers reaching their senior years, about one third of the population is over the age of 50. There are now more people over 65 years of age than at any other time in history.[30] The challenge for the church will be to meet the needs of both elderly and young, a relevant senior ministry and a vibrant youth ministry.

Future Church

We are facing a more educated future than ever before. In 1950 only 18% of older Americans had a high school diploma, and 4% had at least a four-year college degree. In 1998 67% of older Americans had high school diplomas and 25% had at least a bachelor's degree.[31] People are more educated and expect more from a pastor's message. You can no longer make bold statements and expect people to just believe it "because I said so!"

To be relevant we must communicate truth in contemporary terms. Evaluate your ministry for relevance. Ask yourself, "Am I repeating clichés and giving pat answers without thoughtful consideration?" Work at making your preaching, teaching, and witnessing applicable to the experience of people's lives. Hour-long sermons seldom hold the attention of our congregations. The "remote-control" generation will turn you off after 3 minutes or less if you don't grab their attention. Use visuals, use drama, ask for Bible readings, and involve people in your preaching!

To be relevant we must communicate truth in contemporary terms.

People are seeking reality in a plastic world. No doubt this is partly the reason for the success of the numerous *reality shows* on television. It is an opportune time for the church to rise to the challenge and declare a living Christ to a dying world. This is the ultimate reality show – living life for an eternal prize!

Future Church

Many challenges and changes face the church at this crucial juncture in time. Throughout the centuries of church history God has faithfully preserved His Word and the Gospel message. The power of the message has not diminished with the transitions of time and may confidently be expected to weather the storms of passage again in this eventful millennium. However, the church cannot rest on its traditions and past formal liturgy to communicate the faith to a changing generation. The Gospel message must be made to speak in relevant terms to contemporary society. To exist as a vital force in the 21st century, we must adjust to meet the challenge of a changing culture. For the church to have a future, we must be the *Future Church!*

> The Gospel is like a submarine: it does not sit on the water, but moves deep down in the depths of the ocean – and if that water is not deep enough for it, then it moves away to other regions...[32]

[1] Paul K. Conkin, *American Originals: Homemade Varieties of Christianity* (Chapel Hill: The University of North Carolina Press, 1997), 322.
[2] Ibid., 321.
[3] "Pentecostalism Catches Fire," *Life Magazine*, Fall 1997, 57.
[4] C. Peter Wagner, *Look Out! The Pentecostals are Coming* (Carol Stream, IL: Creation House, 1973).
[5] Global Harvest Ministries; online; accessed May 4, 2004; available from http://www.globalharvestministries.org/index.asp?action=peter.
[6] Harvey Cox, *Fire from Heaven: The Rise of Pentecostal Spirituality and the Reshaping of Religion in the Twenty-First Century* (Reading, MA: Addison-Wesley Publishing Company, 1995), 15.
[7] Vinson Synan, ed., *Aspects of Pentecostal-Charismatic Origins* (Plainfield, NJ: Logos International, 1975), 1.
[8] Vinson Synan, *The Century of the Holy Spirit: 100 years of Pentecostal and Charismatic Renewal, 1901-2001* (Nashville: Thomas Nelson, 2001), ix.
[9] Ibid.
[10] John David Ashcroft, a member of the *Assemblies of God* and the son of a Pentecostal preacher, was appointed to the post of Attorney General of the United States by George W. Bush and won confirmation February 1, 2001 after a bitter fight by political opponents. He previously served as a two-term Governor of the state of Missouri as well as a term in the U.S. Senate.
[11] The term *glossolalia* is derived from the Greek *glossa*, "tongue" and *lalia*, "manner of speech," i.e. "speaking in tongues."
[12] U.S. Department of State's Bureau of International Information Programs; online; accessed June 14, 2004; available from http://usinfo.state.gov/products/pubs/muslimlife.
[13] Ibid.
[14] Ahmad Al-Helew, letter to Dear respected brothers and sisters in Islam, October 14, 2002, South Bay Islamic Association (SBIA), San Jose, CA.
[15] John Naisbitt, and Patricia Aburdene, *Megatrends 2000* (New York: Avon Books, 1990), 297.
[16] Brian Duncan, *Slow Revival*, "Things are gonna change" (Word/Epic, 1994).
[17] Acts 17:28 – The passage from Acts (vs. 24-28) may be especially applicable. Paul addressed a philosophically pluralistic culture in Athens. It may be helpful to remember that the disciples were not ministering in a Christian nation!
[18] The Spirit is seen as rivers, John 7:38-39; wind, John 3:8, Acts 2:2; dove, John 1:32.

[19] Erwin Raphael McManus, *An Unstoppable Force: Daring to become the church God had in mind* (Loveland, CO: Group, 2001), 65.
[20] Ibid.
[21] Leonard Sweet, *Soul Tsunami: Sink or Swim in then New Millennium Culture* (Grand Rapids: Zondervan, 1999), 27.
[22] Leighton Ford, *Christianity Today*, "Up & Comers: A Letter to Future Leaders"; Christianity Today, Volume 40, Issue 13, November 11, 1996; Magazine online; accessed January 24, 2003; available from http://www.christianitytoday.com/ct/6td/6td016.html
[23] Lyle E. Schaller, *Innovations in Ministry: Models for the 21st Century* (Nashville: Abingdon Press), 47.
[24] Mountain House, The Best of Yesterday, the Brightest of Tomorrow; online; accessed June 21, 2004; available from http://www.mountainhouse.net/index2.html.
[25] Samuel R. Chand and Cecil Murphy, *Futuring: Leading your church into Tomorrow* (Grand Rapids: Baker books, 2002), 17.
[26] Michael L. Brown, *Revolution in the Church: Challenging the Religious System with a Call for Radical Change* (Grand Rapids: Chosen Books, 2002), 40-41.
[27] Ibid., 44, citing Watchman Nee, *The Normal Christian Church Life* (Anaheim: Living Stream Ministry, 1980), 169.
[28] Chand and Murphy, 15.
[29] Ibid., 34.
[30] Ibid., 66.
[31] Ibid., 74-75.
[32] Mbiti, John S. *"Christianity and African Culture."* Kenneth Aman, ed., *Border Regions of Faith* (Maryknoll, NY: Orbis Books, 1987), 391.

Chapter 2

From Fugue to Chorus

By Laura Payne

Laura Payne, B.A., B.M.Ed.

An alumna of *Christian Life College* with a Bachelor of Arts degree in Christian Music, Laura Payne spent two years on the faculty of *Indiana Bible College* before returning to *Christian Life College* as Dean of the Department of Christian Music in 1996. While teaching in Indianapolis, she completed a Bachelor of Music Education degree from *Butler University*. She is a candidate for the Master of Music degree in Music Education from the *University of the Pacific*, Stockton.

As a missionary child raised in Greece, she brings a broad perspective to her teaching and ministry. An accomplished musician and vocalist, Laura has produced and performed on several recording projects. For the past three years, she has designed and administrated the *Heart of Worship* conference, an annual event of the music department of *Christian Life College*.

From Fugue to Chorus
By Laura Payne

A brief history of the development of music ministry and the lessons that emerge from its study

Although the Pentecostal message traces its roots to the Day of Pentecost as recorded in Acts chapter 2, Pentecostal organizations, as a whole, have not yet reached the century mark and thus are still in their infancy when placed in a larger historical context. The "newness" of oneness organizations means that we are sadly lacking a body of historical and philosophical writing. Although there are theological writers that are working quickly to fill in the gap of our church histories and doctrinal papers, many branches of Christian service remain largely unexplored by formal research or study. Most non-theological texts proffered by oneness authors fall into the category of inspirational writing or church self-help books, which provide practical tips in friendly packages.

The ministry of music is one particular vein which remains vastly unexplored. With the prominence given to music in our church structure, I wish to suggest that we are sadly lacking in educational resources and systematic research to guide not only the musician himself, but to also guide pastors and leaders in their decisions regarding the music department. The research I am speaking of needs to go far beyond the instrumental method books that are becoming increasingly popular, and reach into Biblical study and carefully documented histories and research. Without writings of this nature, we will lose our ability to trace our journey and learn from the lessons of the past. This essay will briefly trace the rise of music ministry, offering suggested areas for historical research that exist. Then I will explore several trends that exist in the music ministry of the United Pentecostal church, illuminating some potential points for future discussion.

Historical Development

The development of music ministers, as we currently know them, is a valuable history to investigate and is one that still remains largely unexplored. The following history is sketchy, at best, but serves to lay a foundation for the present climate of music ministry.

In some ways, church organists and choral directors of the Baroque period—such as J.S. Bach—could be considered the early models of music ministry as we know it; these men were employed by a church to provide music and lead choral groups in preparation for the weekly liturgy. Unlike other well-known composers who would follow in the Classical and Romantic periods, Bach's devotion as a musician was to the church alone.

> Bach was from first to last a church musician. At the height of his fame, he left the only secular position he had ever held, as Capellmeister of the

court of Prince Leopold. He chose instead an obscure position as Cantor at a church in Leipzig, where he would again be cloistered in his unacclaimed but beloved world of church music.[1]

It was common for Bach to compose a new chorale each week, the text chosen from a passage that aptly suited the message. Martin Luther and the Reformation had gifted the world with more than a theological revolution; Luther had been a musician with vibrant opinions about music, strongly advocating that hymns should be sung in the vernacular, the language of the people. Bach was among those who took this challenge to heart and composed chorales in the German language.

It was common for Bach to compose a new chorale each week, the text chosen from a passage that aptly suited the message.

Congregational singing gradually replaced the more formal performances of the church chorale, worshippers integrated with liturgy, and soon it became the norm for churches to provide hymnbooks for their parishioners. It is important to understand the significance of the hymnbook to the church of the 1800's. Much like possessing your own copy of the Bible, the hymnbook represented the living nature of the gospel, taken from the hands of the priest or cantor and placed in the eager hands of the layman. It represented a living and breathing gospel. The parishioner no longer needed to remain distant from his God.

However, as a side consequence, the hymnbook eliminated some of the need for the professional choral director. And, as classically trained musicians began writing in genres that were no longer religious, the schism between trained musicians and church musicians began. While certain denominations continued to employ musicians who composed for the Mass or high liturgy, many religious groups did not maintain high standards of music performance in their congregations. In the New World, music education was grossly neglected and a significant number of children in early American settlements received little or no music training. American education as a whole was in a state of disarray, and it was not until 1837 that, through the efforts of Lowell Mason, music education received any attention in public schools.[2] While some religious groups cultivated a high level of music performance, such as the Moravians,[3] most religious groups in the New World were operating musically at a level considered far beneath that of European composers writing in the classical tradition.

The nineteenth century saw the advent of the "gospel song," so named after P.P. Bliss's hymn book entitled *Gospel Songs* (1874) and Ira Sankey's *Gospel Hymns and Sacred Songs* (1875). This musical tradition, which began as Sunday school and Camp Meeting songs, was influenced by popular secular vocal and band music, such as that composed by Steven Foster and John Philip Sousa. The American revivals of the 1800's, characterized by revivalists such as Dwight Moody, propelled this genre to prominence.[4] The wave of camp meetings that sprung up in urban America required a music that was singable, simple in lyric content, and catchy to the common ear. In the churches that were to give birth to the Pentecostal movement, music was moving farther away from the formal traditions of European choral church music.[5]

Pentecostal Music

Those individuals who transitioned from other denominations into Pentecost in the early 1900's carried with them the simple repetitive refrains of the gospel hymn, having already left well behind the formal structure of liturgical music. Most selections that exist in Pentecostal hymnbooks, including the current hymnbook of the United Pentecostal Church International (UPCI), *Sing Unto the Lord,* are not historically classified as hymns, but are rather part of the broad genre of "gospel songs."

The UPCI took this genre, fueled with the working of the Holy Spirit, and built a musical climate comprised of rote singing, spontaneous by nature, known for its passion and enthusiasm, and generally unapologetic for its lack of musical training. There are exceptions that existed; one should consider the picture portraying a large church orchestra from the 1930's that was displayed until recently in the halls of Calvary Apostolic Church on Greenwood Avenue in Columbus, Ohio.[6] Or the well-developed choral and instrumental program of the 1950's and 1960's led by Wendell C. Gleason while teaching at the Apostolic Bible Institute, St. Paul, Minnesota. His program included a school orchestra as well as an outstanding brass ensemble and choir.

It was not until the 1970's and 80's that the idea of hired music ministers began to take root in UPCI churches. The offering of quality music programs at UPCI endorsed Bible Colleges had much to do with building credibility towards music as a viable ministry, worthy of remuneration. A natural partnership sprang up between churches across the country and those Bible Schools offering music education. It became common for pastors to look towards the yearly crop of graduates for qualified choir directors, piano players and music ministers. Although the majority of churches are still not able to employ a full-time music director, most pastors are of the mindset that the music department is important and that talented personnel are to be coveted.

Historical Insights

There are several valuable observations that emerge from this brief summary of the development of music ministry in the Pentecostal movement. The many trails of historical music research that remain yet untouched by

Oneness Pentecostal writers become quickly evident. Consider the following three historical research avenues, emerging from the dialog above, that beg to be explored:

The first launching point for further research would be to catalogue the repertoire of gospel songs carried into the early Pentecostal organizations. What songs easily became part of our formative repertoire, and what songs, if any, were rejected for theological or stylistic reasons? Which hymnbooks were adopted by early Oneness Pentecostals? What songs were chosen by the compilers and why?

Although I have, of late, heard various people use the term "Pentecostal music," to refer to a style of music that is free-spirited, hand-clapping or foot-stomping in nature, and slightly southern-gospel oriented, it is my opinion that we do not possess a unique repertoire of music exclusive to our movement or even to Oneness theology. Instead, Pentecostal music has always been an eclectic collection of repertoire drawing from a multitude of sources. Greater research regarding our repertoire as a whole would prove valuable.

Generally, our movement is sadly lacking in demographic studies that explore trends and statistics in our churches. There are a multitude of demographic studies that would be of benefit to the music ministry. These include research into the level of education of music ministers, pastor preference surveys to increase awareness between pastors and music ministers, and demographic studies on those involved in local church leadership.

A third point of research that emerges from this brief history is the need to gather written histories of great musicians that have been part of Oneness organizations throughout the 20th century. The musical legacy of men such as Wendell C. Gleason in our movement remains largely undocumented. Consider Cleveland M. Becton, a dynamic classically-trained piano player in his day, who continues to play for congregations before beginning his sermon. Then there is the story of Jean Urshan who was once asked to participate in a radio talent show, which she rejected to dedicate her voice to the Lord.[7] These are stories that need to be recaptured before they are lost forever to time. What about the histories of those musicians such as Dottie Rambo who started their musical journey within the ranks of our fellowship? What lessons do their lives offer to young music ministers today? Can we learn from the past and stem the tide of gifted musicians who abandon their Oneness heritage? What are we doing wrong? What are we

> Can we learn from the past and stem the tide of gifted musicians who abandon their Oneness heritage?

doing right? The lessons of our past offer valuable insight as we pursue ministry in this contemporary culture.

Philosophical Insights

There are several philosophical points that emerge from our historical reflections. The first is that music has been and will continue to be closely tied to theology. Luther saw vernacular singing as an imperative part of moving from mere religiosity to genuine faith. The great Methodist Awakening that led to early Pentecostal experiences encouraged the writings of singable tunes with repetitive melodies to accompany outdoor camp revivals. The pastor who fails to work hand-in-hand with his music ministry is cutting off a viable expression of his theology!

The hunger of each generation for revival and spiritual renewal easily manifests itself through music. Skepticism and concern for "where music is heading now" is not a new cry. But we must acknowledge that many of the great spiritual awakenings that led to the Pentecostal outpouring of the early 20th century were accompanied by distinct changes in musical style! I am not advocating radical music for the sake of musical style alone, but I believe that we cannot afford to squelch the cry for revival and spiritual renewal when it exists. We must listen beyond genre alone and encourage those who are seeking a deeper experience with God.

Trends in Performance Style

Only by looking at church music as it has progressed over the past 300 years do we see larger trends in performance style. Although our current musical climate is perhaps more removed in its harmonic structures and voicings from the formal choral traditions of Bach and other classical composers, in many ways we have come full circle in our desire for musical complexity. I would suggest that music has become increasingly intricate in the past twenty years. The implementation of jazz harmonies into the gospel song has created a repertoire that far surpasses the early gospel hymns in structural complexity. Furthermore, as our movement has matured so have the standards for performance been raised.

This is an important point for leaders in our movement to grasp. The level of "acceptable craftsmanship" has greatly increased. Musicians must be able to perform at a higher level of proficiency in order to meet an acceptable standard for a church today. No longer are we content with musicians who "plunk out" the I, IV and V chord on the grand piano. Instead, musicians must be well-versed in rhythmic motives, be able to handle increasingly complex syncopations and be able to play with a band. Technology is becoming a common part of our weekly services, and musicians must learn how to incorporate sequences, drum loops and electronic instruments through MIDI. We have come to a strange crossroads of complexity, far from the days where everyone in the church was invited to open their hymnbook and proceed to the platform to sing in the "choir."

I am a huge advocate of progress, and I appreciate the higher standard of excellence that has been promoted in our musicians. However, the danger of this trend is that many of our traditional musicians no longer feel that they have something to offer the local church, and feel intimidated by the skill of the new generation. Young musicians are now mentored by other young musicians, instead of receiving apprenticeship from older musicians of the church.

Pastors, in their desire to have "the best music in town," are propagating this trend, without giving thought to the long-term implications for their local church. A significant number of young musicians are offered levels of great responsibility, often "snatched up" by pastors before they even complete any formal musical training. Lack of training does not bode well for our future. While young musicians may have keen awareness of the contemporary pulse of music culture, their lack of training brings with it several potentially destructive consequences:

> **Lack of training does not bode well for our future.**

1. Young people who have not been properly mentored will not demonstrate adequate spiritual leadership that is necessary to create a

vital and sustained music program. Music ministry is ordained by God as part of the Levitical priesthood. It is a high calling that should not be entered into lightly.

2. Young musicians often lack people skills. Most musicians do not realize that music ministry is 80% about people and only 20% about music! Wisdom to make accurate decisions towards ministry matters comes only through experience and careful mentoring.

3. Musicians who are not formally trained are not equipped to serve as educators on a local level, because they have not been exposed to adequate models of music education. If a church wishes to build a long-term, healthy program that continues to refresh itself there must be systematic training at all levels, beginning with the youngest children of the church.

4. Musicians who are placed in levels of responsibility for their talent alone often become absorbed with their own performance and stylistic preferences, and isolate other musical genres that would bless the local congregation.

These four points are intended to highlight some of the weaknesses that can exist when a young musician is given a level of high responsibility based on talent alone. Solutions to these issues include supporting educational opportunities for young musicians, creating mentoring relationships between older music directors and younger leaders, as well as finding room for traditional musicians to guide young musicians on the local church level. A pastor should carefully evaluate the social, spiritual, and educational gifts of any person placed in leadership over the music department.

The greatest philosophical question that we must address is to examine the music ministry and determine if we are effectively reaching our world for the cause of Christ. The United Pentecostal Church International, which I mention simply to represent one Oneness organization, has approximately three million members worldwide and one million in the United States. Furthermore, growing populations of what once were considered minorities are changing the demographics of our churches in America. These statistics should be closely evaluated by the music ministry and pastors who are providing vision to the music department. Sadly, we have few music ministers who have developed a global perspective for their music. It bears further research to explore what types of musical genres should be used to facilitate powerful ministry on a global level.

> **May our vision increase as we draw from the strength of yesterday and accept the challenges of tomorrow.**

It is my hope and prayer that the historical points of interest and philosophical topics presented in this paper will not be seen as a statement of finality in any one area, but will simply be the beginning of greater dialogue and writing concerning music ministry. May our vision increase as we draw from the strength of yesterday and accept the challenges of tomorrow. It is my desire to see the music ministry work in tandem to pulpit ministry, so that we may see an unprecedented display of God's power in these last days.

---

[1] Patrick Kavanaguh, *The Spiritual Lives of Great Composer* (Nashville, TN: Sparrow Press, 1992), 13.

[2] Lois Choksy, Robert M Abramson, et al., *Teaching Music in the Twentieth Century* (Englewood Cliffs, NJ: Prentice-Hall, 1986), 5.

[3] The Moravians developed outstanding music programs in their New World colonies of Salem, NC and Bethlehem, PA. Their music included not only well-developed choral works but trombone choirs and stringed instruments. It is interesting to note that the Moravians are a religious group to which some have attributed speaking in other tongues. This mention of tongues is found in records of Indian Missionary work in the Ohio region. It would be a valuable study to examine their hymn collection for evidence of the doctrine of the infilling of the Holy Ghost.

[4] For more information on the gospel song, see the dissertation by Paul Hammond: *Music in Urban Revivalism in the Northern United States, 1800-1835*, (Louisville, KY: Southern Theological Baptist Seminary, 1974).

[5] The Holiness Movement is closely tied to the early days of Pentecost. Their hymn repertoire still remains largely undocumented, although there are several writers that are exploring this vein of hymnody. Several composers that are included in the *Sing Unto the Lord* hymnbook are classified as Holiness writers, including William J. Kirkpatrick.

[6] The church James Stark currently pastors in Columbus was once pastored by W.T. Witherspoon, chairman of the Pentecostal Assemblies of Jesus Christ (prior

to the merger that formed the United Pentecostal Church International). The church orchestra was without a doubt one of the strongest of its day and included a large string section.

[7] Joanne Swim, Jean L. Urshan, *Our First Lady—Chosen by God* (St. Louis, MO: Harvestime, 1991), 45. This interesting tidbit is only briefly mentioned in this pictorial biography of Jean Urshan.

Chapter 3

*The Use of the Hebrew Scriptures
in the New Testament:
An Introduction to Canonical-
Compositional Hermeneutics*

By Daniel L. Segraves

Daniel L. Segraves, B.A., M.A., Th.M., Ed.D.

After earning a diploma in Bible and Theology from *Western Apostolic Bible College* in 1967, Rev. Daniel Segraves was ordained by the *United Pentecostal Church International* and became the Director of Promotions and Publications for the General Sunday School Division in 1968. He has also served as the Junior High editor for Word Aflame Publications, minister of Christian Education for the *First Pentecostal Church* in St. Louis, Missouri, and pastor of *First Pentecostal Church* of Dupo, Illinois.

While pastoring, Segraves completed the Bachelor of Arts degree in Theological Studies from *Gateway College of Evangelism*. After being recruited for the faculty of *Christian Life College* in 1982, he earned the Doctor of Education degree from *California Coast University*, the Master of Arts degree in Exegetical Theology from *Western Seminary*, and the Master of Theology degree, also from *Western Seminary*. He is currently completing the requirements for the Ph.D. in Renewal Studies with a concentration in Biblical theology at *Regent University*, Virginia Beach, Virginia.

Dr. Segraves is the author of numerous Christian books and commentaries and is a popular speaker at seminars and conferences. His daily teaching program *"Principles for Today's Christian"* can be heard on the KYCC radio network. He is married to author Judy Segraves. In addition to his duties as President of the college, Dr. Segraves teaches several courses each semester, and is an adjunct professor at the Urshan Graduate School of Theology.

The Use of the Hebrew Scriptures in the New Testament: An Introduction to Canonical-Compositional Hermeneutics

By Daniel L. Segraves

The Problem

A comparison of New Testament (NT) references to their Old Testament (OT) sources invites the question as to whether the meaning found by the NT writers is the meaning intended by the authors of the OT sources.[1] The problem is such that Bultmann argued for complete theological discontinuity between the OT and NT.[2] In Bultmann's opinion, we need to "give up the naïve, traditional meaning of prophecy and fulfillment, and go on indeed to ask if we may legitimately speak of prophecy and fulfillment at all."[3] In Hasel's view, Bultmann's mistake is "to approach and criticize the NT's method of quotation from the point of view of modern literary criticism."[4] Instead, "one must maintain that the NT quotations presuppose the unity of tradition and indicate keywords and major motifs and concepts in order to recall a larger context within the OT."[5] Hasel's point is that in Bultmann's failure to see any anticipation of NT persons or events in the OT and in his view that the NT authors read meaning into the OT texts,[6] Bultmann read Scripture anachronistically; rather than recognizing the ancient literary devices that shaped the meaning of the OT, he read the OT through the lens of modern literary techniques. Bultmann's reading focused narrowly on individual verses quoted or alluded to in the NT rather than on the larger inter-textual context; he did not take into account the canonical-compositional issues that lend meaning to smaller portions of the text.

A Possible Solution: Canonical-Compositional Hermeneutics

This chapter suggests that the idea of discontinuity between the NT authors and their OT sources is due to an excessively narrow perspective on OT theology. This narrow perspective fails to read the OT as a book. Instead, it is read as a collection of books or, worse, as a collection of books lacking internal integrity. This literary fragmentation strips the OT of cohesion and thus of any unity of focus. This approach, unprecedented until the eighteenth century, has its origins in the rise of historical criticism.[7] The vision of historical criticism was to discover the supposed history behind the text; the reconstruction of the events that gave birth to the text became more significant than the exploration of the text itself.[8] The OT, which had previously been read from Genesis 3:15 onward as anticipating the coming of a messianic figure, was transformed into little more than an historical account of past figures and events.

In contrast to the hermeneutical methods associated with historical criticism, a canonical-compositional hermeneutic focuses on the final shape of the TaNaK. This final shape is viewed as intentional and informative. Scholars working in this field view the canonical context as more determinative of meaning than the original author.[9] There are four common emphases of canonical criticism: (1) Since the church has received the Bible as authoritative in its present form, the focus should be on that canonical form rather than on a search for the sources behind the text; (2) the text must be studied holistically to determine how it functions in its final form; (3) the theological concerns of the final editor(s) must be explored; and (4) in later texts, the canon provides clues in the use of earlier biblical texts.[10]

> **The idea of discontinuity between the NT authors and their OT sources is due to an excessively narrow perspective on OT theology.**

Brevard Childs asserts that "the lengthy process of the development of the literature leading up to the final stage of canonization involved a profoundly hermeneutical activity on the part of the tradents."[11] The idea is that those who were involved in the preservation of literary tradition shaped the text in such a way that the shape influences interpretation.

The first thing noticed in a comparison of NT references to their OT counterparts is that all references are not created equal. Moyise suggests that it is "helpful to distinguish between quotations, allusions and echoes."[12] Citation formulas usually indicate quotations. Key words characterize allusions. Verbal links that do not seem to reflect authorial intention to specify an OT source may be described as echoes.[13] In spite of these variations, canonical-compositional hermeneutics emphasize continuity between the testaments.[14]

An Illustration of Canonical-Compositional Hermeneutics

In order to illustrate an application of canonical-compositional hermeneutics, we will explore Paul's use of Psalm 14 in Romans 3:10-12.[15]

The similarities between Psalms 14 and 53 are such that Psalm 53 is often thought of as merely a doublet, revision, or corruption of Psalm 14.[16] One proposed reason for the differences is that Psalm 53 appears in the *Elohistic* book of the Psalter,[17] whereas Psalm 14 appears in the *Yahwehistic* portion of the Psalter.[18] Another proposed reason is that Psalm 53 is a revision of Psalm 14 done in the northern kingdom and reflecting a more generic view of the identity of God.[19] There are, however, more differences between the two psalms than the name by which God is identified.

From the perspective of canonical-compositional hermeneutics, Psalms 14 and 53 are intentionally placed in the Psalter in their precise locations. This placement reflects the overall messianic theme of the book. The context in which each psalm is found informs intentional and inspired differences between the two. Each serves an intended purpose in advancing the theme of the Book of Psalms.

In the context leading up to Psalm 14, the focus is on Israel's covenant relationship with יְהוָה [*Yahweh*] and specifically on sinfulness within the covenant community. The nature of the sin is an attempt to thwart God's messianic purpose through David.[20] That this is the covenant community

> From the perspective of canonical-compositional hermeneutics, Psalms 14 and 53 are intentionally placed in the Psalter in their precise locations.

is demonstrated by the use of the name יְהוָה in each psalm leading up to and including Psalm 14. The use of יְהוָה in Psalm 14 in contrast to the use of אֱלֹהִים [*Elohim*] in Psalm 53 is significant. As Mitchell points out, "A tendency can be discerned in the Bible to use the name *Yhwh* in contexts referring to God's mercy and steadfast love (Exod. 33.19; 34.6), and the term *Elohim* in contexts referring to his judgment or universal sovereignty (Exod. 22.7, 8 [8, 9]). This was recognized by rabbinic interpreters, for whom it was a fixed interpretational principle."[21]

In the immediate context of Psalm 53 (Psalms 51-54), the focus is on sinfulness in the Gentile community and God's judgment of Gentiles. The specific sin is the same as the sin of Israel; Gentiles also seek to frustrate the messianic promise.[22] That this is the Gentile community is demonstrated by the use of אֱלֹהִים in the psalms that provide the immediate context for Psalm 53 (i.e., Psalms 51, 52, 54[23]). It is also demonstrated in that all of the psalms in this context have to do with Gentiles in some way: Psalm 51 with David's sin with a Gentile woman;[24] Psalm 52 with David's betrayal to Saul by the Gentile Doeg; Psalm 53 with the Israelite Nabal behaving as a Gentile;[25] and Psalm 54 with David's betrayal to Saul by the Gentile Ziphites.[26]

From the perspective of canonical-compositional hermeneutics, Psalm 53 is intentionally placed in the Psalter immediately after Psalm 52.[27] When read with intentionality in mind, Psalm 53 demonstrates the judgment of God upon the Gentile world. In order for it to serve its literary purpose, the psalm was amended by inspiration[28] to identify God exclusively as אֱלֹהִים rather than יְהוָה, God's covenant name revealed to Moses in conjunction with the deliverance of the people of Israel from Egypt.[29] Together with this development, other changes were made to affect a shift in the psalm's focus. These changes can be seen as follows:

There they were in great fear, for God is with a righteous generation. You would confound the purpose of the poor, but the LORD is his refuge (Psalm 14:5-6).[30]

There they were in great fear where there was no fear, because God scattered the bones of him that camps *against* you. You have put *them* to shame, because God has rejected them (Psalm 53:5).

In Psalm 14, Gentiles are in great fear because God is with Israel (i.e., a righteous generation). These Gentiles may seek to confound the purpose of the poor (i.e., Israel), but יְהוָה is the refuge of the poor. Psalm 53 reveals a subtle but significant difference: A new fear has gripped the hearts of the Gentiles. It is not just because God is on the side of Israel, but because God is aggressive in destroying the Gentiles. God scatters the bones of those who seek to destroy Israel. Whereas in Psalm 14 the Gentiles seek to confound Israel, in Psalm 53 Israel shames the Gentiles. Indeed, God has rejected those who intend to harm Israel. The ultimate harm that could come to Israel would be the destruction of the messianic hope.

> **The ultimate harm that could come to Israel would be the destruction of the messianic hope.**

In both psalms Israel and the Gentiles appear. But in Psalm 14 the focus is on God's covenant with Israel; in Psalm 53 the focus is on God's universal authority over the entire world of unbelievers.

Both psalms conclude with a nearly identical focus on Zion theology:

> Who will give the deliverance of Israel from Zion? When the LORD returns the captivity of His people, Jacob will be glad; Israel will rejoice (Psalm 14:7).

> Who will give the deliverance of Israel from Zion? When God returns the captivity of His people, Jacob will be glad; Israel will rejoice (Psalm 53:6).

The only difference between these verses is that Psalm 14 identifies God as יְהוָה and Psalm 53 as אֱלֹהִים. Thus, Psalm 14 focuses on the return of Israel from captivity from the perspective of the covenant God had with Israel. Psalm 53 focuses on the return from the perspective of God's universal authority over all peoples of the world, including those who held Israel captive.[31]

Regardless of the perspective, salvation comes out of Zion.

Regardless of the perspective, salvation comes out of Zion. The Psalter's Zion theology begins in Psalm 2:6; the messianic King, the Son, has been set by God on the holy hill of Zion. Throughout the Psalter, messianic deliverance is seen as originating in Zion. Although the Psalter recognizes the judgment of God upon the holy city due to the sinfulness of its inhabitants, the psalms are oriented toward a bright future beyond the Babylonian captivity, a future involving the restoration of Zion and the establishment of a literal kingdom governed by the Messiah from His headquarters in Zion [Jerusalem].[32] Their references to Zion as the source of deliverance tie Psalms 14 and 53 together with the messianic theme of the Psalter.

It is significant that Paul, in a series of quotes from the OT to demonstrate the sinfulness of the Jewish people, uses the LXX version of Psalm 14:3, not Psalm 53:3.[33] That this was intentional is indicated by the context in which Paul uses this quote.

In Romans 1:18-32, Paul establishes the universal sinfulness of Gentiles, whose revelation he portrays as limited to creation and conscience. But in Romans 2:1 – 3:19 he establishes the universal sinfulness of Jews, whose revelation included the written Scriptures. Thus he appeals to a psalm that, in its original context, described the same ethnic group he sought to portray. Paul's use of Psalm 14 rather than Psalm 53 is an apparent acknowledgement of the significance of the context created in the composition of the Psalter. In his treatment of the universal sinfulness of Gentiles, Paul quotes no OT text. In his treatment of the universal sinfulness of Jews, Paul quotes three OT texts[34] before the lengthy reference to the OT in Romans 3:10-18. This suggests that rather than reading meaning into the OT, Paul uses the OT carefully, contextually, with due regard for the preservation of meaning. Certainly he could have found references to endorse the idea of Gentile sinfulness. But since his point is that their revelation was limited and did not include the written Scriptures, Paul does not appeal to the written Scriptures to demonstrate their sinfulness. But when he seeks to establish the sinfulness of the Jews, Paul appeals to an abundance of Scriptures. He is careful, however, to use those Scriptures that are contextually about Jewish sinfulness, even if other very similar Scriptures are available (e.g., Paul uses Psalm 14 rather than Psalm 53).

Strengths and Weaknesses of Canonical-Compositional Hermeneutics

The strengths of canonical-compositional hermeneutics include its high view of inspiration, its apparent literary validity, and its relevance to the use made of the Hebrew Scriptures in the NT.

Canonical-compositional hermeneutics extend inspiration beyond individual words and immediate contexts to the full scope of Scripture. Inspiration is not merely in-textual or even inner-textual; it is inter-textual. We might call it "macro-inspiration" as opposed to "micro-inspiration." The final work commonly referred to as redaction is identified as composition and included in the process of inspiration. Inspiration is not attributed to scribal copying. Sailhamer explains:

> A canonical theology of the OT is based on the canonical text of the OT rather than a critically reconstructed one.

Because our approach begins with a theological premise, that is, the verbal inspiration of Scripture, we believe the biblical text must be taken as authoritative, that is, as canonical.[35]

Sailhamer recognizes the value of biblical criticism and the challenges associated with distinguishing between the work of an author, a redactor, an editor, and a scribe, but points out that "the canonical OT theology which we are proposing, does not have to resolve the question of an original text—even though we hold it to be possible to do so. A canonical approach to OT theology focuses its attention on the shape of the OT text at the time of the formation of the Canon."[36]

Although after the time of Christ fluidity existed in the order of the canonical books in both the Jewish and Christian traditions, Roger Beckwith points out that "the earliest evidence is of a single agreed order, and since this order is referred to by Jesus, it provides a measure of confirmation that the closing of the canon had already taken place in Jesus's time.[37] Walter Brueggemann suggests that the three-fold shape of the Hebrew Scriptures described by Jesus as the Law of Moses, the Prophets, and the Psalms (Luke 24:44) is anticipated in Jeremiah 18:18.[38]

The literary validity of canonical-compositional hermeneutics is apparent in view of the discoveries made by scholars currently working in this field. Although an exploration of these literary discoveries is beyond the scope of this paper, Sailhamer's comments are helpful:

By paying careful attention to the compositional strategies of the biblical books themselves, we believe in them can be found many essential clues to the meaning intended by their authors—clues that point beyond their immediate historical referent to a future, messianic age. By looking at the works of the scriptural authors, rather than at the events that lie beyond their accounts of them, we can find appropriate clues to the meaning of these biblical books. These clues . . . point to an essential messianic and eschatological focus of the biblical texts. In other words, the literal meaning of Scripture . . . may, in fact, be the spiritual sense . . . intended by the author, namely, the messianic sense picked up in the NT books.[39]

This is not to say "that the authorially-intended meaning can only be ascertained when the books are read in a certain order. Rather, the order is *instructive*, helping [us] to see what is already there in the text."[40]

The relevance of canonical-compositional hermeneutics to the use of the Hebrew Scriptures in the NT has to do with the NT writers' apparent recognition of how the meaning of specific texts is influenced by their literary context.[41] After a discussion of the way the literary shape of the Pentateuch influences the reading of Deuteronomy 18 in the direction of eschatological messianism, Sailhamer points out that this is precisely the way the text is read in Acts 3:22; 7:37. Thus,

When the NT writers appear to us to read their OT typologically and counter to its "historical" sense, we may have to exercise more caution before drawing the conclusion that they have misread their Biblical texts. When viewed from the standpoint of the final shape of the canon, their reading of the Bible may be much closer to the original intention than our own. . . . Such a reading may be more in harmony with the intention of the original authors of the Hebrew Scriptures than that of our own historical reconstructions.[42]

The weaknesses of canonical-compositional hermeneutics include as yet unanswered questions about the authority of the LXX and, since the NT is equally inspired with the OT, questions about the order of books in the NT.

The fact that more than one-half of the quotations from the OT in the NT are from the LXX invites the question of the authority of the LXX. Since it is a translation, is the LXX authoritative only insofar as it is quoted in the NT? Does the fact that the LXX order of books does not follow the Hebrew canon invalidate the idea that the relationship between the books informs interpretation? In James Barr's view, errors in the

LXX became the basis for theological claims in the NT, thus invalidating the concept of an inerrant text: "The New Testament did not build its interpretation upon the Old Testament text as it originally was or upon the meanings which it was originally intended to convey. . . . Thus some very important features in the New Testament owe their entire existence and form to the fact that the Old Testament had been inaccurately transmitted."[43]

Sailhamer recognizes the challenges associated with the theological influence of the LXX on the NT writers, but the issue has yet to be adequately addressed from the perspective of canonical-compositional hermeneutics.[44]

Canonical-compositional hermeneutics claim that the TaNaK order of the Hebrew Scriptures contributes to the meaning of the entire text. But does this hold true for the order of books in the NT? The order of the books was fluid in the earliest days of the Christian church.[45] Childs believes that a basic error is involved, however, in "the assumption that the literature was shaped by historical, literary, sociological, and history-of-religion forces, but that the theological struggle of its tradents with the literature's normative function was insignificant."[46] Instead, Childs agrees with S. Pedersen that the NT canon has theological content and that "certain aspects of the struggle to bring to bear content-oriented norms on the process of selecting and ordering the New Testament writings"[47] is reflected in selected texts.

Conclusion

There is sufficient evidence for the validity of canonical-compositional hermeneutics to merit the investigation of its significance for Pentecostal theology. In Acts alone, there are at least forty-five verses containing direct quotes from the OT.[48] At least twenty-nine of these verses present their OT source as having to do with Christ or with events or persons associated with him.[49] Much of Peter's Pentecostal sermon consists of direct quotes from the OT. These quotes validated Jesus as the promised Messiah and connected the events of Pentecost with specific prophecies.

Although Paul quoted directly from the OT when he addressed Jewish audiences,[50] it is significant that he did not quote from the OT when addressing Gentiles. In his sermon at Athens, his only literary source consisted of quotations from the Greek poets Epimenides and Aratus.[51]

If the first apostolic theologians found a rich source of authority for their experiences by reading the OT in a way that reflects values consistent with canonical-compositional hermeneutics, the church in this era may discover an inexhaustible wealth of theological insight from the same practice.

---

[1] A classic point of debate is the use of Isaiah 7:14 in Matthew 1:23. Matthew claims that the promise of Isaiah 7:14 is fulfilled in the virginal conception of Jesus. But it is common to read Isaiah 7:14 as a promise to Ahaz, who was dead long before the birth of Christ. As Moyise notes, "Jewish scholars have always protested that many of the cited texts have been taken out of context. . . . If this is a prediction of the birth of Jesus 700 years hence, then it makes utter nonsense of the story being narrated in Isaiah" (Steve Moyise, *The Old Testament in the New: An Introduction* [*The Continuum Biblical Studies Series*; ed. Steve Moyise; London and New York: Continuum, 2001], 2-3).

[2] Gerhard Hasel, *Old Testament Theology: Basic Issues in the Current Debate* (4th ed.; Grand Rapids, MI: William B. Eerdmans Publishing Company, 1991; reprint, 2001), 173.

[3] Rudolf Bultmann, "Prophecy and Fulfillment," in *Essays on Old Testament Hermeneutics* (ed. Claus Westermann; ed. English translation, James Luther Mays; trans. James C. G. Greig; 2nd ed.; Richmond, VA: John Knox Press, 1964), 74.

[4] Hasel, *Old Testament Theology*, 176.

[5] Ibid.

[6] See Bultmann, "Prophecy and Fulfillment," 51-55, 72-75.

[7] A survey of historical criticism's rejection of the pre-Enlightenment Christological understanding of the Hebrew Scriptures is offered by Ronald E. Clements, *Old Testament Prophecy: From Oracles to Canon* (Louisville: Westminster John Knox, 1996), 49-61.

[8] John H. Sailhamer, *Introduction to Old Testament Theology: A Canonical Approach* (Grand Rapids: Zondervan Publishing House, 1995), 36-85.

[9] Mary C. Callaway, "Canonical Criticism," in *To Each Its Own Meaning: An Introduction to Biblical Criticisms and Their Application* (ed. Steven L. McKenzie and Stephen R. Haynes; Louisville: Westminster John Knox Press, 1993), 126. See also Rolf Rendtorff, *Canon and Theology: Overtures to an Old Testament Theology* (Minneapolis: Fortress Press, 1993), 51, 55.

[10] Ray Lubeck, "An Introduction to Canonical Criticism," Evangelical Theological Society Papers 1995 (Portland, OR: Theological Research Exchange Network), 1-2.

[11] Brevard S. Childs, *Biblical Theology of the Old and New Testaments* (Minneapolis, MN: Fortress Press, 1992; reprint 1993), 70. The word "tradent" refers to someone who studies or preserves tradition and is increasingly used by scholars in place of "traditionist." This may be due to possible confusion between "traditionist" and "traditionalist."

[12] Moyise, *The Old Testament in the New: An Introduction*, 5.

[13] Ibid., 5-6.

[14] The variety of approaches by which continuity is emphasized is represented by Brevard S. Childs, *Biblical Theology: A Proposal* (Minneapolis: Fortress Press, 2002); Bruce K. Waltke, "A Canonical Process Approach to the Psalms," in *Tradition and Testament: Essays in Honor of Charles Lee Feinberg* (ed. John S. and Paul D. Feinberg; Chicago: Moody Press, 1981); Walter C. Kaiser, "The Single Intent of Scripture," in *The Right Doctrine from the Wrong Texts?* (ed. G. K. Beale; Grand Rapids: Baker Book House, 1994); G. K. Beale, *John's Use of the Old Testament in Revelation* (Sheffield: Sheffield Academic Press, 1998); Scott A. Swanson, "Can We Reproduce the Exegesis of the New Testament? Why Are We Still Asking?" *TJ* 17:1 (1996): 68-76; Ray Lubeck, "An Apologetic for Canonical Shaping of the Old Testament (TaNaK)," Evangelical Theological Society Papers 2000 (Portland, OR: Theological Research Exchange Network); and John H. Sailhamer, *Introduction to Old Testament Theology*.

[15] The connection between Psalm 14 and Romans 3:10-12 is explored in Daniel Lee Segraves, "An Application of Canonical-Compositional Hermeneutics to Psalms 14 and 53" (Th.M. thesis, Western Seminary, 2003).

[16] See Anthony Tyrell Hanson, *Studies in Paul's Technique and Theology* (Grand Rapids, MI: William B. Eerdmans Publishing Company, 1974), 22; W.O.E. Oesterley, *The Psalms: Translated With Text-Critical and Exegetical Notes* (London: S.P.C.K., 1962); James L. Mays, *Interpretation: A Bible Commentary for Teaching and Preaching, Psalms* (Louisville, KY: John Knox Press, 1994).

[17] The term "Elohistic Psalter" refers to Psalms 42-83. In these psalms, God is ordinarily referred to by the word אֱלֹהִים rather than יְהוָה. It should be noted, however, that יְהוָה does appear frequently in the Elohistic Psalter and that אֱלֹהִים often appears in the Psalter outside of Psalms 42-83.

[18] See Willem A. VanGemeren, in *The Expositor's Bible Commentary*, vol. 5 (gen. ed., Frank E. Gaebelein; Grand Rapids, MI: Zondervan Publishing House, 1991), 388.

[19] See Mitchell J. Dahood, *Psalms II: 51-100* AB 17 (Garden City, NY: Doubleday & Company, Inc., 1968), 19.

[20] That sinfulness has infected the covenant community may be seen in that much of the focus of this section of the Psalter, beginning with Psalm 3, has to do with rebellion within the house of David.

[21] David C. Mitchell, *The Message of the Psalter: An Eschatological Programme in the Book of Psalms*, JSOTSup 252 (Sheffield: Sheffield Academic Press, 1997), 172.

[22] An examination of the contexts of Psalms 14 and 53 may be found in Segraves, 22-54, 75-93.

[23] Psalm 54 does have one use of יְהוָה in David's prayer, but this use is disputed by Kraus. See Marvin E. Tate, *Word Biblical Commentary, vol. 20. Psalms 51-100* (gen. eds. David A. Hubbard and Glenn W. Barker; OT ed., John D. W. Watts; Waco, TX: Word Books, 1990), 45, n. 8.b.

[24] Although Bathsheba's ethnic origins could be debated, Yehoshua Gitay writes, "The name 'Sheba' ('Shua' in 1 Chronicles 3:5) probably refers to a foreign god, which may indicate the family of Bathsheba was of non-Israelite origin" (Paul J. Achtemeier, gen. ed., *Harper's Bible Dictionary* [San Francisco: Harper & Row, 1985], s.v. "Bathsheba"). Bathsheba's father was Eliam (2 Sam 11:3), whose name means "god of the people." Eliam's father was Ahithophel the Gilonite (2 Sam 23:24). Ahithophel means, "My brother is foolish." Ahithophel – Bathsheba's grandfather – was David's counselor, but he betrayed David in the Absalom incident. Even if Bathsheba were Jewish, she was married to a Gentile. This supports the contextual relationship of Psalm 51 with Psalms 52-54.

[25] The idea that Psalm 53 recalls Nabal is based on the observation that the arrangement of Psalms 52-54 follows the order of the events in 1 Sam 21-26. David's betrayal by Doeg is found in 1 Sam 21:7; 22:9-23. Nabal's rejection of David is found in 1 Sam 25:2-44. Psalm 53 concerns the fool, the נָבָל, who lives as if there is no God. Nabal's denial of David's legitimacy (1 Sam 25:10, 11, 22, 38), since David had been anointed by Samuel (1 Sam 16:1-13), was essentially a denial of God. Although Nabal was an Israelite (1 Sam 25:3), he behaved like a Gentile, as suggested by Psalm 53. The background of Psalm 54, concerning David's betrayal to Saul by the Ziphites is found in 1 Sam 26.

[26] Although Ziph belonged to the tribe of Judah (Joshua 15:20-24), those from that area who betrayed David are described as "strangers." Even if they were Israelites, they were behaving like Gentiles. Literally, this conforms Psalm 54 to the general context of Gentile treachery. Dahood is of the opinion that Psalm 54 "distinctly emerges as the supplication of a king for deliverance from his foreign enemies" (Mitchell J. Dahood, *Psalms II: 51-100*, 23.

[27] See Norman Whybray, *Reading the Psalms as a Book*, JSOTSup 222 (Sheffield: Sheffield Academic Press, 1996); Gerald Henry Wilson, *The Editing of the Hebrew Psalter* (Chico, CA: Scholars Press, 1985); J. Clinton McCann, Jr., ed., *The Shape and Shaping of the Psalter* (Sheffield: JSOT, 1993); idem., *A Theological Introduction to the Book of Psalms: The Psalms as Torah* (Nashville:

Abingdon Press, 1993); William L. Holladay, *The Psalms through Three Thousand Years: Prayerbook of a Cloud of Witnesses* (Minneapolis: Fortress Press, 1993); Nancy L. DeClaisse-Walford, *Reading from the Beginning: The Shaping of the Hebrew Psalter* (Macon: Mercer University Press, 1997); David C. Mitchell, *The Message of the Psalter: An Eschatological Programme in the Book of Psalms* (Sheffield: Sheffield Academic Press, 1997).

[28] In his approach to canon criticism, Brevard Childs does not clearly define inspiration or distinguish between the relative value of literary activity and scribal activity. (See Brevard Childs, *Introduction to the Old Testament as Scripture* [London: SCM Press, 1979].) Canonical-compositional hermeneutics, developed more recently, attributes inspiration not only to the original authors, but also to those involved in the final composition of the text. (See, e.g., Sailhamer, *Introduction to Old Testament Theology*, 36-85.)

[29] Exodus 3:14-15; 6:1-7.

[30] All translations are by the author.

[31] The final verse may be an inspired post-exilic addition. If so, Israel was not in captivity when these psalms were originally written. See Norman Whybray, *Reading the Psalms as a Book*, 61; VanGemeren, *The Expositor's Bible Commentary*, 15.

[32] See, e.g., Psalms 48:2; 110:1-2.

[33] That Paul quoted from Psalm 14 rather than Psalm 53 is demonstrated in Segraves, 132-140.

[34] These texts are Proverbs 24:12 (in Romans 2:6), Ezekiel 36:22 (in Romans 2:24), and Psalm 51:4 (in Romans 3:4).

[35] Sailhamer, *Introduction to Old Testament Theology*, 222.

[36] Ibid., 223.

[37] Roger Beckwith, *The Old Testament Canon of the New Testament Church* (Grand Rapids: Eerdmans Publishing Company, 1985), 222.

[38] Walter Brueggemann, *The Creative Word: Canon as a Model for Biblical Education* (Philadelphia: Fortress Press, 1982), 7-10.

[39] Sailhamer, *Introduction to Old Testament Theology*, 154.

[40] Lubeck, "An Apologetic for Canonical Shaping of the Old Testament (TaNaK)," 8. Emphasis in original.

[41] This has been illustrated in this paper by an examination of Paul's use of Psalm 14 in Romans 3:10-12.

[42] John H. Sailhamer, "The Canonical Approach to the Old Testament: Its Effect On Understanding Prophecy," *JETS* 30:3 (1987): 315.

[43] James Barr, *Beyond Fundamentalism: Biblical Foundations for Evangelical Christianity* (Philadelphia: The Westminster Press, 1984), 144.

[44] Sailhamer, *Introduction to Old Testament Theology*, 18, n. 12.

[45] See Authur G. Patzia, *The Making of the New Testament: Origin, Collection, Text and Canon* (Downers Grove, IL: InterVarsity Press, 1995).

[46] Brevard S. Childs, *The New Testament as Canon: An Introduction* (Philadelphia: Fortress Press, 1985), 22.

[47] Ibid.

[48] Acts 1:16, 20; 2:17-21, 25-28, 34-35; 3:22-23, 25; 4:11, 25-26; 7:3, 7, 27-28, 32-35, 37, 40, 42-43, 49-50; 8:32-33; 13:22, 33-35, 41, 47; 15:16-17; 28:26-27.

[49] Acts 1:16, 20; 2:17-21, 25-28, 34-35; 3:22-23; 4:11, 25-26; 7:37; 8:32-33; 13:22, 33-35; 15:16-17; 28:26-27.

[50] Acts 13:22, 33-35, 41, 47; 28:26-27.

[51] Acts 17:16-31.

Chapter 4

Everyone Needs Encouragement and Inspiration from Somewhere

By Judy Segraves

Judy Segraves, A.A.

Judy Segraves has been a minister's wife for over four decades. She has served beside her husband in various roles of ministry. This includes pastoral work, establishing and maintaining a model A.C.E. K-12 school, Bible college administration and teaching for over twenty-two years, and other areas. She began writing many years ago for Sunday school curriculum, then branched out into articles, stories, and eventually put together five books. She has been a first place winner three times in the Word Aflame Writer's contest. Judy is a graduate of *Christian Life College*.

She is the mother of Mark and Sharon and the grandmother of Erin, Danielle, Ethan, Luke, and Christiana. Her husband is Dr. Daniel L. Segraves, president of *Christian Life College*.

Everyone Needs Encouragement and Inspiration from Somewhere

By Judy Segraves

Someone once said to me, "You really are an encourager to people." I felt a little embarrassed and very small. Then along the way different ones would comment on a story or article they had read. "That really spoke to me," they said. "That is exactly how I felt in my situation," one minister's wife commented.

Writing to touch people seems to be a gift the Lord saw fit to entrust to me.

When this volume was in its planning stage, I was asked to add something to it, for the leaders felt inspiring people was a good ministry. For me, inspiring and encouraging others emerges as I write with a personal touch.

I have had some ask me how to begin writing. That is not an easy question to answer. Since we are all different parts of the body of Christ, our skills and gifts will be displayed differently. When one can grasp that, his own particular style of writing can become exciting. It can be exhilarating to birth a story or article for others to read and find food for their soul.

Now take my husband and me. We are examples of two different types of writers. He loves to study and dig out information about doctrine and theology from various angles. He will study for hours and write one paragraph. His paragraph might have a dozen footnotes. I am not a footnote kind of person. I just recently learned how to make a footnote appear on a page using a computer. This was only because a college course I was taking required me to make a footnote. I don't even like footnotes. My husband actually *reads* footnotes!

I write totally from something that pops into my head, or from something that I experienced or felt. A story or theme will suddenly come unbidden, and I am immediately on a roll. I can sit at the computer and finish an article in an hour or two. I feel writing in my heart. I will look at the sentences and laugh or cry sitting in front of the screen full of words. I *feel* the message and hope the reader will feel it also. This is called "writing by inspiration." In a creative writing course, the students were told that if the writer can feel the story, more than likely, the reader will.

The following story gives an example of a person wrestling with hidden guilt and how releasing that guilt can bring freedom. What better person to write about this subject than the guilty culprit. That, of course, is me.

Settling an Old Score

I was hoping I'd never see him again. Though I had tried numerous times to locate him, it seemed he was always out of town. In a way, I was relieved.

It had been forty years since the altercation that still troubled my conscience. It haunted me periodically. There was new determination in my spirit as I learned of his whereabouts. As a matter of fact, he was located not far from the place it had all happened.

My husband and I were returning to our childhood hometown to speak at some special meetings in the church we attended as teens. While visiting with a distant relative of mine, I learned that my seventh grade gym coach and history teacher was right there in town. He had opened a pizza parlor upon his retirement from teaching.

It was time to settle an old score that kept popping up too often.

I took my husband along, and we walked into the door of the restaurant. The smell of pizza and my nervousness made me nauseated. My hands were perspiring. I hoped I didn't look as nervous as I felt to the customers sitting at the green covered tables.

One of the waitresses told us my old teacher came in only during the rush hours at noon and at dinnertime.

We made plans to return just before my husband's first speaking session that evening. We waited until most of the dinner crowd would be away and made our second entrance. Some of the nervousness had dissipated by now. My former teacher had gone away to pick up some needed supplies, and we missed him again. We couldn't hang around or we'd be late for our own meeting.

As the evening wore on, I forgot about the coach. He could wait a little longer. After all, he had waited forty years.

The next day, once again I made myself ready to do what I had wanted to do many times in the past. When it was close to the noon hour, my husband and I made our way back to the pizza parlor. I saw him standing behind the counter, and my stomach did a couple of U-turns.

He was older for sure, but so was I. A lineup of about fifteen middle-school kids hovered about the cash register giving orders and handing him money. They stood around teasing each other, pushing on each other, and making calls on cell phones. Times had changed a lot of things. I saw myself as a youth when I looked at them. The coach was still working with kids as he had been doing when I first met him.

We sat out of the way and waited. He was expecting me but couldn't take a break until everyone had been served. I watched him and dreaded when he would be done.

All too soon, he came over and said, "Well, it's so good to see you again." I knew he really didn't recognize me. "Tell me all about what you've been doing these past few years," he added.

I interrupted and introduced my husband. Then we talked of family and told each other how many children and grandchildren we now had. Then I decided it was time to get to the reason for my visit.

"Coach, I wanted to come by to see you because I have something that has been bothering me for over forty years." He had a rather puzzled expression that mixed in with his broad smile.

"I know you probably really don't even remember me. I was on your seventh grade girls' basketball team and I was also in your history class." When I told him what year it was, he said it had been his first year to teach school. He was twenty-two at the time.

> **He had a rather puzzled expression that mixed in with his broad smile.**

I proceeded. "You may think I'm a little strange to do this, but I have come to apologize to you. It is for something that happened one day in class." He looked even more bewildered. "We were taking a final test and my girlfriend and I had decided she would help me out if I got stuck on a question. She was always the smart one in class. I would tap her chair that sat right in front of me, and she would gently move her paper over so I could see it.

Well, I did it. Just as I looked at her test paper, you saw me."

I cleared my throat and went on. "'That will be twenty points off your score!' you said in a very deep, commanding voice." His eyes twinkled. "I won't ever forget the sentencing I received for trying to cheat on a test. I still have the report card that states I didn't do my own work on the final. I almost flunked history because of that one mistake!

> I almost flunked history because of that one mistake!

"The reason I am here is to apologize and tell you how sorry I am for doing that. It has bothered me all these years. I am now married to a preacher. I don't know what got into me! It has never been my habit to cheat or do anything wrong on purpose. I have really tried to be a good Christian since I was a girl.

"I am sorry," I said again.

He smiled even wider. "Hey, don't worry about it. All of us have done things like that and wished we hadn't. I'll tell you what. You can just consider that your slate has been marked clean."

We talked a little bit more before we said our "good-byes."

I couldn't get his words out of my mind. "Your slate has been marked clean." It was a good way for a teacher to say it.

But he isn't the only one who gives me a clean slate. Every once in a while, I have to go to God and ask His forgiveness and tell Him I am sorry for my wrongdoing. But just like the coach, He sends me away feeling good again because He, the greatest Teacher of all time, keeps erasing things that should not be on the slate of my life.

That story is one many can relate to. The human race deals with similar problems. The situations might vary, but the heart of man has to continually deal with greed, pride, or moral impurity. The lesson: *There is always peace in forgiveness.*

Another sample story follows. It should cause the reader to think about examining his own life before placing judgment on others.

Stained Glass Windows

Since we lived right beside the church my husband pastored, I made it a practice to wash the glass entry doors before each service. It wasn't a chore, really. I rather enjoyed the quietness of working on them. I might have been called the "doorkeeper" by some.

For many months during the year, the weather was nice enough for the neighborhood children to play their games on the street in front of the church building. To my dismay, they often made a game room of the entrance into the building. After all, it did have a nice porch to protect them from the sun and rain. Cars were pushed along make-believe freeways, and dolls were cuddled close to little girls' hearts as they sat on the welcome mat and rocked back and forth.

One little boy, who lived across the street, made it a habit to cup his hands around his eyes, set them on the glass doors, and peer inside. It was hard to see through the tinted glass, so he would change positions several times. This left a smear of dirt and grime from his sweaty, little-boy hands.

Over and over it happened. I might be in the church doing something, and I'd see him peering in the door. He always left his mark. I knew when he had been there.

> **At first it didn't bother me. I just kept cleaning the doors.**

At first it didn't bother me. I just kept cleaning the doors. Even through the week when there was no service, I would find myself getting the window spray and some paper towels to erase the smudges. But then I began to let it bother me. Why didn't his mother make him play on his own porch?

I was standing on the platform one day and looked back toward the entrance just in time to see the four-year-old leave a large stain.

"Another mess! Some more smudges! I will have to clean it again!"

A small voice seemed to whisper, "Yes, the same way I keep cleaning smudges from the windows of your heart."

Tears welled up in my eyes and spilled over. I thanked God for the many times he had washed me clean. The little boy had served to remind me of His cleansing power. "Though your sins be as scarlet, they shall be as white as snow" (Isaiah 1:18).

I continued to wash away the stains as before, but my attitude changed. It became a reminder to me.

Could you feel the writer's heart melt when she realized her own shortcomings? An inspirational story sends out a message to the reader. The lesson: *Don't be critical of others, but be certain that your own life is pure.*

It was Mark Twain who said, "Write about what you know about."[1] Many of his writings were taken from his experiences in childhood. It is a fact that many writers have branched out to put things into print that they have not studied out or researched. In a lifetime, one will come across something that is simply not fact. Those who are born to research will write from their findings. Those born to tell tall tales from an expanded imagination thrill readers worldwide. Those who write from experiences tap into another type of reader. As there are many different kinds of writers, so are there many different kinds of readers. There is something for everyone.

Even this chapter within this book might give a point or two that will enlarge someone's knowledge. Writing is to tell someone something you are exploding to share. The following article will give some tips to the reader about writing. Writing is one way to inspire. It is a ministry also. You might be the next one to pen (type) a masterpiece. You may be surprised at what is hidden within, that is just aching to get out to help and inspire someone!

So You Want to Write?

I guess everyone at one time or another thinks about becoming a great writer. It might be after reading a good book or an article that spoke to the heart or left you with warm feelings. You ask yourself, "Now, why couldn't I have written that?"

But there are some people who don't just talk about writing, they actually sit down and do it. If you feel writing is something you wish to do, I want to give just a few guidelines as to some of the procedures.

It isn't a hard thing to do; you just do it. There are four basic questions every prospective writer needs to ask.

1. Why do I want to write? Here's why. It is to tell someone what you know. If there is something you have learned, experienced, or read about, it is easier to tell more people if you put it on paper and in a language they understand. Going from person to person to tell them your message is far from feasible. It only makes good sense to write it down and pass it around.

2. What will I write? That will depend on what you know. You don't have to be really intelligent to write. I know that from experience. If you have something burning inside that you want to share with others, the simple thing is to put it on paper. No one has had quite the same experiences you've had, although most experiences are very similar. Automatically you have a "listening ear" as the reader relates to what he reads. It's the comparison mode. For example, if you write about being lost in the woods, the reader shifts into your shoes and begins to feel what you felt. The terror and agony become very real. The reader feels a real sense of relief when he knows the writer has found his way home.

A poem written on paper can be preserved and passed down through the centuries. A poem spoken aloud would in time not even resemble the same poem. Dropped words and phrases and even added words and phrases would eventually make the original not original at all.

> A poem written on paper can be preserved and passed down through the centuries.

Do you know how to do something that others do not know? "How to Repair a Leaky Faucet" is a good bit of knowledge to share with someone who has a leaky faucet.

Maybe you desire to tell others how to live a victorious life. You have found some steps that help you, and writing them down just might help someone else. The list of "what to write" is endless.

3. Where do I write? That will depend solely on you. There is no assigned place. What is good for one writer may not be suitable for another writer. For some, it will be riding thirty thousand feet in the air with a laptop on their knees. Others will recline on a sofa with a yellow legal pad and write with a medium point blue *Bic* pen. Then there will be those who refuse to give up the ever-faithful IBM typewriter. Those who have turned to the modern PC are quickly gaining momentum in the writing field.

Whichever method one chooses to use is entirely up to the individual. But after the thoughts are recorded, they will need to go through a process to be made ready for public consumption. This is where a good editor is valuable.

4. How do I write? This is probably the most important question of all. It will be impossible to write if you haven't mastered the alphabet. And I mean "A" to "Z." It also helps to be knowledgeable in sentence structure.

There is a subject (who or what the sentence is referring to). There is a verb (this is some sort of action that is taking place). There is usually a descriptive word or phrase to help the reader understand what is actually happening to the thing doing the action.

If you can recall the first reading lessons in life, it will be easy to see what I am about to explain. As the writer matures, he is able to "flesh out" his written message.

Let's use the following sentence as an example.

See Dick run. We are told to look at Dick because he is running. Unfortunately, the early reading books did not tell us in this sentence who he was running from, how fast he was running, or why he was trying to get away. Was Dick running after Jane or away from Jane? The key is to build up those sentences so the reader can visualize what is happening.

There has been a great change in writing practices. The very earliest writers chiseled on the sides of caves and other hard-to-get-at places. It was very different from going into the nearest Christian bookstore to find a good book to read. Who would want to find a cave in the dead of winter, climb into it with a torch and read the messages? And who knows what they wrote about. Maybe they recorded a list of the savages who had tried to take away all their wives. Tables of stone seemed a bit more progressive. At least you could haul them around on a wagon.

> **The key is to build up those sentences so the reader can visualize what is happening.**

The creation of paper from leaves, bones and whatever else was pure genius. The writer could actually carry everything under his arm or in a valise. But the greatest invention so far has been the high powered computer. It puts the words down almost before you have had time to think about what you're writing. The spelling and sentence structure correction feature is terrific. It's rather hard to argue with a computer. And sometimes it's so stubborn it won't let you write what you want to write.

> It's rather hard to argue with a computer.

This is only a beginning for the writers of tomorrow. One of my friends, who doesn't type well, bought the most recent computer gadget so he could write quickly while the thoughts were hot in his head. All he has to do is speak to it. He plugged in the little timesaver and set about to test it. Some of his first words that he spoke into the handheld contraption were his name: Arlo Moehlenpah. Immediately, across the computer screen was displayed, "Hi! Old moldy paw!" This could be a problem. Sometimes I really believe the pen and paper will always be the leader in tools for writers. At least ideas can be recorded on paper and tossed into the "Ideas to Write About" file.

You see, it really isn't hard to be a writer. You just write. Psalm 45:1 refers to a ready writer. There are other references to the ready writer. In the Bible it was someone who wrote down the things that needed to be recorded.

Now you know some things about the why, what, where, and how of writing. All you have to master at this point is taking up the pen and becoming one of those "ready writers," one who writes because there is something of great value that needs to be recorded and passed around for everyone to read.

There are many gifts given to the body of Christ. To encourage, to edify, and to strengthen are gifts that can be shared with everyone. If God has blessed you and endowed you with the ability to uplift others, whether by writing or personal contact, don't delay. Use your gift today.

Now that your appetite is stirred a bit for the ministry of writing, let me share some things you can do with a story, article, or book.

Within the United Pentecostal Church International (UPCI) there are many opportunities to have a story or article printed. I have submitted stories to my local church for different bulletins, magazines, or newsletters and they were published. There are many district magazines whose editors are looking for publishable material. Word Aflame Publications at the UPCI headquarters needs stories and articles for Sunday school lessons and take home papers for all age levels. The Youth Division publishes various magazines and has a variety of writing needs. They have a magazine for young people and another for married couples that deals with marriage, the home, and family.

The Women's Division publishes a magazine six times a year and prints stories from various writers.

If you wish to publish a book or booklet, it can be submitted to Word Aflame Press at the UPCI headquarters for consideration. Because they receive many submissions and are able to publish only a few of them, it is sometimes difficult to find a publisher for your book. If a publisher will not take your manuscript and you feel your written material would have a reading audience, you can self-publish. There are many publishers who can do short runs if you wish to make only a few books available. Of course, the fewer you print, the higher the price per book.

> **There is always a person whose life can be helped by reading something written from the pen of the ready writer.**

Some have printed books for just their local church. Others who travel in ministry can take their books and offer them at the various churches where they minister. There is always a person whose life can be helped by reading something written from the pen of the ready writer. If you are leaning toward writing as a part of your ministry, the next time you feel a flash of inspiration, go to your computer and sit down. Take a step of faith and begin. They say that starting a project is the hardest part. That really is true. I can testify to that. But because I sat down and started this chapter, it is now finished and ready for you to read.

---

[1] Mark Twain Entertainment; Online; accessed 4-12-04; available from www.kellys.com/twain.

THE GRACE OF INSPIRATION

Inspiration, elusive angel,
    Why do you kiss at such an inconvenient time?
While I sit and dawdle with an empty page,
    in leisurely moments void of demands,
        your grace is never near.
But when I've thousands of things to do,
    and activity buzzes my cluttered brain,
        you light like a feather in a bated breeze,
            and a flood of inspiration fills my mind and heart
A million ideas for song and verse,
    and themes for literary masterpiece, and art and prose,
        and sermons with powerful points to pen.
And then, why can't you come at will,
    with ordered steps present your understanding,
    let your brilliant fire burn with clarity and flow,
        like oil from a fine tuned pen,
            and script appear upon demand.
No you, like the Spirit who guides you,
    whisper in the wind, lighting where he lists,
        and sets ablaze the desert bush or chariot ride
            and drops his mantle on whom he will.
Inspiration like grace comes not with demand nor design,
    but with delight on some unsuspecting soul.

                --Terry R. Baughman, 2/22/99

Chapter 5

Priceless Presents

By Gayla M. Baughman

Gayla M. Baughman, B.A.

After earning certification in Secretarial Occupations from *Idaho State University*, Gayla Baughman continued her education at *Conquerors Bible College* for two years. She then joined her family in evangelistic ministry, the *Bible Singing Bibb Family*, until her marriage to Terry R. Baughman in 1979. She graduated from *Christian Life College* with a Bachelor of Arts degree in Christian Music in 1999.

Gayla is currently a faculty member at *Christian Life College* where she serves as Academic Assistant, the instructor of several courses, and the faculty advisor of the *Open Door Ministries* women's conference. She is also a member of the *Women of the Word* commission of the UPCI. Gayla is the author of a Pentecostal guide to social etiquette, *Christian Social Graces,* as well as other publications. The Baughmans are planting a church in nearby Pleasanton, California.

Priceless Presents
By Gayla M. Baughman

A warm sensation of nostalgia settled in the room. A young college student sat across from me and expressed her intense desire to be used of God. The memories of my own youthful searching reverberated with her words, "I don't know what to do with my life. I don't know what my gifts are, so I don't really know where to start in ministry." I smiled as though some inspiration balanced on the edge of our conversation, but in reality, I pondered her words wondering what to say.

How about you? Which side of the desk are you sitting on? Are you saying with a sigh, "Those were the days"? Do you have memories of lazy days that distanced you from dreams and ambitions like an eternal stretch of tomorrows reaching for the horizon of the future? How long has it been since you hoped there was something God could use in you? How many years have passed? Do you feel like an old worn out shoe that has been cast in the closet corner, not sure of how much usage is left? Or are you sitting on the opposite side with a future of opportunity stretched out before you and no clue where to start?

As the young lady in my office and I continued to discuss her dilemma, the Lord stepped in and gave us an idea. As we began working through her gifts and talents, I became the student. We worked through every positive trait imaginable to categorize her gifts and talents. As time passed, I began to realize something very important about availability in the Kingdom of God. The revelation came like a street light in the distant fog, and it gradually brightened as we progressed until it was a brilliant glow of luminosity. God can take just about *anything* we have to offer and use it for ministry! We don't have to be *accomplished in every area* God wants to use us. On the contrary, sometimes God surprises us with a challenge to dig in to a new task, one we have never done before, just to see how willing we are to do "whatever" for God. Or perhaps God wants us to learn some new skills to broaden our horizons and give us a diversified base to work from, making us more versatile and adaptable.

Being available is a key ingredient to opportunities in ministry.

I have heard it said, "God is not looking for ability. He is looking for availability." Some people who are not born leaders find themselves *leading* contrary to their lack of self-confidence in their ability to lead. Do you know someone who seems to attract leadership jobs? Are you one of those people? Do you have a "may I help you" look? Maybe you are an "I'll follow through" or "you can depend on me" person. To some, jobs always seem to fall in their laps whether qualified or not, not necessarily lucrative ones, but important, challenging, and rewarding ones just the same. Whatever it is, you find yourself serving on committees, heading up programs, and leading meetings with no clue how you got there. Perhaps there is something to this "availability" thing. Being available is a key ingredient to the opportunities in ministry.

Others have a passion to work for God but the opportunities seem to detour right around them to someone else. It seems there is always someone else who is more talented, or more spiritual. It may be noted that if God had wanted an orator to speak his word, Moses would have never stood before Pharaoh and led the Children of Israel out of Egypt. If God waited for someone more spiritual, David would never have been king. If God would have waited for someone with more experience, a young handmaiden named Mary would never have been overshadowed by the Holy Ghost and given birth to the Messiah. If God were looking for someone with more courage, Peter never would have had the chance to proclaim Christ on the Day of Pentecost after an embarrassing denial at the trial. God is not looking for people who fit the mold; He is looking for people ... *to mold*.

> **God is not looking for people who fit the mold; He is looking for people ... *to mold*.**

Are you willing to step out of the security of inferiority and allow God to use you in any capacity? Wow! If you can do that ... you may be the next leader, or the next voice He uses. It doesn't really matter if you have great gifts or not; He is looking for the gift of yourself ... unreservedly given to use in His kingdom. This sounds a lot like "availability" again, doesn't it? It could be that the first step in being used in ministry is availability.

Gifts vs. Talents

Let's get back to the young lady sitting patiently in my office. She was ready to be used of God. She felt that the process of "availability" was finished; now she wanted to go on to the next level. Next, we focused on her talents and gifts. We worked through her desire to help people. We separated gifts from talents and decided that some talents are not gifts.

This is the way we described a talent. A talent is an ability or opportunity God gives you. You have the choice to use it, to help it grow as a skill, or to let it lie dormant and just sort of fade away. An area of interest may be a seed of talent. Although you may not be good at this talent, you enjoy it enough to spend time perfecting and growing in that area.

A gift is different than a talent. A gift is something that is extra-ordinary. It is something that comes naturally without any effort. Gifts cost very little or nothing. Gifts are freely given by someone else. A talent, on the other hand, is something you work for and nurture to see it grow. A gift grows naturally. God gives us gifts that are just waiting to be used.

The "gifted" children in school are those who seem to enjoy studying. These children thrive in the environment of learning. Thus, they learn easier, faster and with less effort than the general population of students. I know a woman who is gifted musically. She has perfect pitch, plays the organ for relaxation and doesn't feel intimidated by others or exhausted after performing either for enjoyment or church. She is gifted. An extraordinary ability of her gift is "perfect pitch." She can hear a note in her head and touch the organ or keyboard on that exact note. She can hum a note to help an *a cappella* choir find the key much like someone else might use a tuning fork to perform without accompaniment. Her gift is obvious because of this extraordinary skill, but not all gifts are so obvious.

> There are diversities of gifts, but the same Spirit. There are differences of ministries, but the same Lord. And there are diversities of activities, but it is the same God who works all in all. But the manifestation of the Spirit is given to each one for the profit of all (1 Corinthians 12: 4-7 NKJ).

Identifying your gifts

If you are unsure where your gifts are, there are some helpful tools to direct you. Personality tests are available to help you identify your strengths and weaknesses.[1] When you realize your strengths, it is easier to understand why you enjoy some things and avoid others. A weakness can be overcome after a time, but for starters your strengths are the obvious targets in locating your gifts.

Spiritual Gifts

Then, of course, there are spiritual gifts that God has given to each of us. In the book *Women Mentoring Women,* Vickie Kraft describes a spiritual gift as "a supernatural capacity freely and graciously given by the sovereign God at the time of a person's salvation, enabling that person to minister to others for the purpose of accomplishing God's work."[2]

There are many gifts in the Word of God. The opportunities to be used in His kingdom are endless! Although this is not a comprehensive list, some of the characteristics of gifts listed in the Bible are as follows:[3]

1 Corinthians 12	**Ephesians 4**	**Romans 12:1-13**
Administration	Evangelist	Encouraging
Apostles	Pastor	Exhortation
Discerning of Spirits	Teaching	Giving
Faith		Helpers
Healing	**1 Timothy 2:1**	Hospitality
Interpretation	Intercession	Leadership
Knowledge		Mercy
Miracles	**Romans 10:15**	Serving
Prophecy	Missionary	
Tongues		
Wisdom		

Vickie Kraft characterizes the process of finding your spiritual gift this way:[4]

1. Start with prayer, individually and with others. Ask God to reveal your gift.
2. Study what the Bible has to say about spiritual gifts.
3. Ask God's people what they observe about your abilities and effectiveness.
4. Examine your strongest desires or interests.
5. Look for an opportunity to serve in that capacity.
6. Allow God to confirm by experience and the feedback of others.
7. Notice the area in which you experience joy and ease in exercising your gift with results beyond expectations.

Finding your talent

What do you enjoy doing? Painting, playing, or praying? How about singing, swinging and sewing? Check off the words that you think you may be interested in:

- Arts & Crafts
- Baby sitting
- Computer graphics
- Design
- Drama
- Drawing
- Education
- Elderly care
- Photography
- Playing an instrument
- Praying
- Public Relations
- Reading
- Sewing
- Shopping
- Singing

- Electronics
- Encouraging
- Exercise
- Graphics & Design
- Hospitality
- Nursing
- Painting
- Speaking
- Sound & Equipment
- Support groups
- Teaching
- Traveling
- Writing
- Other _____

Use your individualized list to help focus on a ministry. For example: if you enjoy *exercise,* you may want to start an exercise and weight loss program and host it in your church. Not only will you be able to create an atmosphere of fellowship for the women in the congregation, but you can also use this as an outreach to invite others as well. The key is to think "ministry" when you focus on your talents.

If you feel you need a little more instruction in an area of interest, enroll in your local community college or consider adult night classes. The opportunities are endless. You can get involved!

Priceless presents

Do you feel inadequate if you are not multiple-gifted? God specialized in using ordinary people like Moses, David, Mary, and Peter for extraordinary missions. He finds some sort of satisfaction in making the simple supreme and the ordinary ornate. What you may think is an old ordinary talent may be a gift wrapped in a plain, brown paper bag. But once that plain wrapping is untied and the contents exposed—what an exquisite product! God has refined your gifts just for the giving! You, a priceless instrument, unwrapped and ready for debut! He chooses to use the gifts he gave you in the beginning to bring about a special purpose in your life. He chooses to allow you to perfect the gift, and in His time He exposes the priceless jewel.

When I am shopping for a birthday present for one of my children, I look for one that fits my special recipient perfectly. The most fulfilling experience is to watch one of them tear into my gift excitedly and exclaim, "This is just what I wanted!" or "I love it! I will use it." They are never timid about claiming my gift for their own. They know if it is wrapped and presented to them, it is theirs immediately. Open your heart to the spiritual gifts that are available to you. God is extending these priceless presents with a big bow attached to the top. All you have to do is accept the gift He is giving you. It doesn't matter that it may take you a little time to open it or to find out which gift He has given you. This is all a part of His plan, but once you have opened it enough to reveal the gift, thank Him for it and start using it. I am sure you will be pleasing the Father who gave the gift to you.

> **Open your heart to the spiritual gifts that are available to you.**

[1] Explanation of the personality temperaments and self evaluations are available in the following resources: Timothy LaHaye, *Spirit Controlled Temperament* (Wheaton, Illinois: Tyndale House Publishers, 1993) or Florence Littauer, *Your Personality Tree* (Nashville: W Publishing Group, 1986).
[2] Vickie Kraft and Gwynne Johnson, *Women Mentoring Women* (Chicago: Moody Publishers, 2003), 60.
[3] List of gifts taken from various sources including, C. Peter Wagner, *Finding Your Spiritual Gifts* (Ventura, CA: Gospel Light, 1995); Vickie Kraft and Gwynne Johnson, *Women Mentoring Women* (Chicago: Moody Publishers, 2003); *The Woman's Study Bible* (Nashville: Thomas Nelson, 1995).
[4] Kraft, 62.

Chapter 6

Involvement:
A Christian's Responsibility

By Daryl Rash

Daryl Rash, B.A., M.A.

Daryl Rash is a graduate of *Western Apostolic Bible College* where he earned the Bachelor of Arts degree in Bible and Theology. He has served as pastor in Coolidge, Arizona; Carmichael and Grass Valley, California. He was ordained by the *United Pentecostal Church International* in 1966. In 1993 he earned the Master of Arts degree in Exegetical Theology from *Western Seminary*.

Daryl Rash, and his wife Carol, answered the call to foreign missions in 1974 and served under appointment to Indonesia, Austria, Holland, and Germany, during their years as missionaries. Rash came back to the United States as a faculty member at *Christian Life College* in 1983. Except for three years when he returned to Germany as the Administrator of the *Weisbaden School of Bible*, he has continued to teach courses in missions and multi-cultural evangelism. He serves as the Dean of Missions. He is also on staff as an associate pastor at *Christian Life Center*, Stockton, California.

Involvement: A Christian's Responsibility

By Daryl Rash

There is perhaps no other subject as controversial as the Christian's position in society. We realize that we can do nothing without the leading of the Holy Spirit, and we do not want to detract from or minimize the influence of God's Spirit in this world. We also are aware that God Himself chose, "...by the foolishness of preaching to save them that believe" (1 Corinthians 1:21). The Lord spoke to His disciples, saying, "Ye are the light of the world" (Matthew 5:14). Again He said, "Ye are the salt of the earth: but if the salt have lost his savour, wherewith shall it be salted?" (Matthew 5:13).

When we look at church history, we must ask ourselves if the church has lived up to the expectations of the commands of our Lord. How successful have we been? Could the church have been more successful in reaching the lost?

The Lord, in His plan, left the church in the world for a purpose. That purpose appears to be twofold: first, "...for the perfecting of the saints" (Ephesians 4:12), and second, "go ye into all the world and preach the gospel to every creature" (Mark 16:15). It is the purpose of this chapter to examine the more popular views of Christian involvement and to form a biblical position for reaching our world.

Separatism

This view of withdrawal from society started during the time of the early church fathers. In the *Evangelical Dictionary of Theology*, R. E. O. White said, "In the apostolic church, the essence of sanctification was a Christ-like purity; in the patristic church, withdrawal from the contaminations of society."[1]

Where the apostolic church radiated a Christ-like purity, the patristic church began to manufacture a simulated sanctification by isolating itself from an active place in society. Believers began to look upon the isolated position as a place of purity, or a sign of sanctification.

This attitude of separation from society was not new. Paul stood up and proclaimed that he was a Pharisee, as was his father. The word *Pharisee* meant separate. Paul was not ashamed of his training as a Pharisee and was merely stating how he had been trained. William L. Coleman discussed the Pharisee in *The Pharisee's Guide to Total Holiness*, and said,

They could wear the title (Pharisee) well since they prided themselves in their denunciation of impure and ungodly elements. Physical separation was of paramount importance. Functional holiness was considered evidence of personal piety, and Lev. 11:44-45 was a central passage.

Their detractors were also happy to use the term but only as a burlesque wit. They considered the Pharisees as a bunch of holy freaks too pious to touch the common man. To them Pharisaism represented a flock of self-righteous prigs.

Whatever the origin of the title, they wore it as did Paul, with dignity. They considered their priorities close to the heart of God.

The Pharisees had no greater task than to protect and propagate the laws of God. Their methods for accomplishing this may seem strange and yet, at the same time, may tell us something about ourselves. The zeal to respect and follow the Scriptures has led people to do odd things—things that they never saw as strange or unusual.[2]

The Pharisees were not insincere, nor did they knowingly or purposely change the Scriptures. Their purpose was to live so completely righteous as to make it impossible to break the law of God.

This same attitude or spirit of separation appeared very early in the history of the church. It is difficult to determine exactly when, but according to C. T. Marshall, in the *Evangelical Dictionary of Theology*, the trend towards monasticism can be traced back to the very beginning of the church. Marshall says that early Christian monastics drew their spiritual strength from the following Scriptures: concerning poverty, where Jesus spoke to the rich young man and told him to "go thy way, sell whatsoever thou hast, and give to the poor" (Mark 10:21), and also when Jesus referred to "the narrow way" (Matthew 7:14). Later celibacy probably came from Paul's teaching on marriage, "I say therefore to the unmarried and widows, it is good for them if they abide even as I" (1 Corinthians 7:8). Marshall traced the record on monasticism back to the second and third centuries. He said,

> The first monks of whom we have a good record represent an extreme phase in the evolution of monasticism. These are the so-called desert fathers, hermits, living in the eremitical style in the deserts of Egypt, Syria, and Palestine. Enraged by sin and fearful of damnation, they left the towns for a solitary struggle against temptation. Some, like Simon Stylites, lived very exotic lives and became tourist attractions. More typical was Anthony of Egypt (250-365), whose commitment to salvation led him back to the community to evangelize unbelievers. His extreme asceticism deeply touched the sensibilities of the age.[3]

These teachings led to the developing and building of monasteries and convents where dedicated people felt they were safe from the temptations of the world and could devote their lives to God.

These early monks and nuns did physical labor, provided charitable services, and performed the duty of safeguarding the Scriptures. The monasteries became popular and by the twelfth century became the recipients of large land grants. The monks became very rich, and those attracted to them were less than righteous. With the decline of the original order of monks, other reformed orders appeared. The last successful revival of monasticism was in the Middle Ages, when the Dominicans and Franciscans appeared. Francis of Assisi was the best known and represented not only the monastic ideal but also Christian idealism.

The Protestant Reformation, the enlightenment, and twentieth century secularism brought an end to the popularity of the monastic order but not the end of separatism.

> **Pietism was actually a recurring tendency within the church to return the church to the practicalities of Christian life.**

Shortly following the Protestant Reformation, Philipp Jakob Spener took a major step towards reviving the church. Spener is known as the father of Pietism. Pietism was actually a recurring tendency within the church to return the church to the practicalities of Christian life. The church had grown formal, the leaders had become insincere, and the church was filled with fighting between different theological factions. The Thirty Years' War, which was in reality a religious war, developed doubts about the church in general. Spener's efforts brought about reform in the church. M. A. Noll listed four general traits of pietism in the *Evangelical Dictionary of Theology:* 1. Its experiential character; 2. Its biblical focus; 3. Its perfectionist bent; 4. Its reforming interest.[4] In spite of the need for the reforming work of Spener and the needed results of pietism, some fears of its opponents were realized. Noll listed them as:

> At its worst the pietistic tendency can lead to inordinate subjectivism and emotionalism; it can discourage careful scholarship; it can fragment the church through enthusiastic morality; and it can underrate the value of Christian traditions.[5]

These items referred to by Noll are still problems the church faces today. We don't want to overlook the four general traits of pietism referred to above. We want to remember that pietism encouraged a return to the Scriptures and encouraged the people to find an intimate fellowship with God.

Other groups followed in the years to come: at first there were Moravians, Quakers, and Mennonites; and eventually there were Baptists, Methodists, and Pentecostals. They were marked with fervor, zeal, and a desire to return to the precepts of the apostolic church.

Harold L. Bussell, in *Lord, I Can Resist Anything But Temptation*, explained that since the time of Christ, sincere Christians have tried to protect themselves by building walls of protection and separation. Monasteries separated from family and friends; vows of silence were intended to separate from lying tongues. Abstinence from certain foods and beverages, and even celibacy, became widespread. Bussell said:

> Many of these attempts to flee temptation through separation from the "world" are not intrinsically misguided. But however much distance we put between ourselves and the "world" the self cannot ward off the intrusion of lust, greed, envy, and hate. However far we flee, or however completely we separate, the self is there. If we understand and accept this truth, it can help set us free from unbiblical and always disappointing attempts to merely flee "the whole mess," or simply separate ourselves from a world "going to hell."[6]

Jesus gave us the proper admonition concerning our position in the world when He prayed, "They are not of the world, even as I am not of the world. Sanctify them through thy truth: thy word is truth. As thou hast sent me into the world, even so have I also sent them into the world" (John 17: 16-18).

Secularism

Perhaps the greatest danger to the church is the danger of secularization, which was defined in the

Evangelical Review of Theology, January, 1986, by Klaus Bockmuehl, in his article titled, *"Secularization and Secularism: Some Christians Considerations."* Bockmuehl defined secularization as, "...the withdrawal or emancipation of social institutions, world views, and individual lives from instruction by, or responsibility to, ecclesiastical or divine authority."[7]

Secularism can be traced back to the Protestant Reformation at which time the ecclesiastical lands and estates were returned to certain individuals. This was a direct result of the age of monasticism in which the monks were considered Christians and all other believers were hardly considered in the church. There developed a clear line between the church and the secular. This marked the end of unlimited power of the Roman Church. This all came about because of the excesses of the church system prior to the Protestant Reformation.

The purpose of secularization was to turn man from the church to humanism, to free man from the authority of the church, and ultimately from God. It was not the intention of the reformers to turn men from God and His commandments, but to correct excesses in the Roman church. Bockmuehl explained this clearly when he said:

> We therefore have to distinguish throughout between two types of secularization, between emancipation from ecclesiastical tutelage, and withdrawal from one's responsibility to the Judgement of God. The former is the intention of

Reformation, the latter the program of more recent centuries. Only the latter is an unlimited proposition, and can thus be called secularism.[8]

The move towards secularism, which followed the Reformation, was quite reserved at first. Secular views were considered as private matters and were not discussed in the pulpit. Ministers were constrained from mentioning anything in the pulpit that wasn't in accord with the church's teaching. By the end of the nineteenth century, things had changed.

People felt that this change would bring about great advances in the freedom of the people, an end to oppression, and great steps toward a heavenly existence on earth. Quite the opposite has happened. In Europe, where this all began, there has been the greatest change. World Wars I and II have shown that secularism will not correct the problems of humanity; in fact, the opposite is true. The state churches of Europe have lost almost all their influence. Hundreds of churches in England have closed their doors. Many are used for purposes other than churches. At least one cathedral in England is now used as a Hindu temple. In Germany, the state churches are open, but attendance is very small. Few young people attend the state churches.

When the church's authority and the authority of God are compromised, people turn to other sources for spiritual things. Secularism has not fulfilled the hopes of the people. Europeans have turned to eastern religions and to the occult for fulfillment. Islam has become the fastest growing religion in America. *Hex schules* (witch schools) are a common sight in German towns and at festivals. Covens are meeting in many cities of America, as well as in Europe. In the Netherlands, many old churches have closed their doors.

The lifestyles of people in Europe and America have been drastically affected by secularization. The family unity is disintegrating, values are changing, and morality is at an all-time low.

Jacques Ellul, in *The Subversion of Christianity*, described the condition of Christianity:

> How has it come about that the development of Christianity and the church has given birth to a society, a civilization, a culture that are completely opposite to what we read in the Bible, to what is indisputably the text of the law, the prophets, of Jesus, and of Paul?[9]

This all sounds pessimistic and discouraging, but this is only one side of the coin. This is the result of secularism, and it is not the only trend in the world. Other forces are at work, and we need to be reminded that the

Lord said, "Upon this rock I will build my church; and the gates of hell shall not prevail against it" (Matthew 16:18).

Biblical Position

The Christian of the Bible is far different than the separatist or secular Christian we have been discussing. Jesus had a very different plan for His church. As we have already noted, the Lord declared that He would build a church that would prevail against the very gates of hell. Jesus told His disciples, "But ye shall receive power, after that the Holy Ghost is come upon you: and ye shall be witnesses unto me both in Jerusalem, and in all Judea, and in Samaria, and unto the uttermost parts of the earth" (Acts 1:8). It is clear that the intent of Christ was for the Christian to be active in spreading the gospel. It is also clear that God did not require him to do this alone but gave the Christian power to accomplish what He commanded. The Bible makes us to know that the early believers understood a struggle would be necessary if they were to be successful. Paul, in his teachings to the Romans, listed the trials of the Christian life as tribulation, distress, persecution, famine, nakedness, peril, and the sword, but reminded the believer that:

> ...we are more than conquerors through him that loved us. For I am persuaded, that neither death, nor life, nor angels, nor principalities, nor powers, nor things present, nor things to come, nor height, nor depth, nor any other creature, shall be able to separate us from the love of God, which is in Christ Jesus our Lord (Romans 8:37-39).

With this kind of faith and assurance, the New Testament Christians endured all manner of hardship and yet were victorious in propagating the gospel in their world.

The attitude of the Christians of the New Testament gives us many clues as to their success. They were people of faith. Paul said, "The just shall live by faith" (Romans 1:17). In Ephesians, Paul stressed God's overwhelming provisions. The believer has the fullness of God.[10]

This kind of faith is the reason the disciples had such tremendous growth when the Lord instructed them to go to Jerusalem and wait until they received power from on high. (See Luke 24:49.) One hundred and twenty people were in the upper room in Jerusalem, and thirty years later Christianity was a world religion.[11] The numbers given in the Bible are enough to stagger the imagination! There were one hundred and twenty people in the upper room, and almost immediately, three thousand souls were added to the church! J. Herbert Kane in *A Concise History of the Christian World Mission*, gave the following account of the growth of the church:

> We know that in A.D. 250 the church at Rome supported one hundred clergy and fifteen hundred poor persons. Assuming the population to be not less than one million, Gibbon estimates the number of Christians at fifty thousand. Fifty years later, according to a third opinion, the Christian community numbered one hundred thousand.

Antioch was the oldest and most illustrious church in the east. According to Chrysostom, towards the end of the fourth century Christians accounted for half of the population of five hundred thousand. Gibbon, however, considers this figure too high and suggests 20 percent rather than 50.[12]

How many Christians were there at the end of the third century? No one knows for sure. Estimates range from ten to twenty-five percent of the population of the Roman Empire. The population of the Empire was estimated at between fifty and one hundred million people.[13]

In the fourth century, growth was even more rapid. After Constantine gave his support to the church, people seemed to rush to embrace the new faith. Kane says that the church in Rome reported twelve thousand men, plus the same amount of women and children, baptized in one year.[14]

Why did the early church have such success? Remember Jesus said "ye are the light of the world" and "ye are the salt of the earth" (Matthew 5:13, 14). It is the purpose of Christians to shine their light into the darkness of paganism and to season unbelievers with the salt of their influence. Kane said of the early church:

> Everywhere and at all times they were to be as salt and light. They were to be different from other men, in character and conduct, in manners and

morals, in motives and ideals; only so could they save the sinner, or reform society.[15]

By the year 200 A.D., Tertullian could write:

We are a new group but have already penetrated all areas of imperial life—cities, islands, villages, towns, market-places, even the camp, tribes, palace, senate, and the law-court. There is nothing left for you but your temples.[16]

The Bible shows us a church ordained of God to evangelize the world. We are assured that God will build this church. He has commissioned believers to go and spread light to a dark world and to permeate the world with the salt of the gospel. The Bible makes it clear that this will be done at the price of great suffering. We are also assured that all the fullness of God will be with His church, and He will be the source of all strength and comfort. He has promised never to leave us and also assured us that He will be an ever present help in the time of need.

We have been instructed to separate from the world and not be conformed to it. (See 2 Corinthians 6:17; Romans 12:2.) We have been instructed not to lay up treasures on this earth but rather to lay up treasures in heaven. (See Matthew 6:19-21.) We have also seen that the early believers trusted and were successful in reaching their world. We must reach our world! The only way is to walk in the light of God's Word and be filled with the Spirit, so that we can truly be light and salt to this world.

How Should We Then Live in Our Society?

Here we are, nearly two thousand years since the church was founded. The church has seen days of great spiritual growth, as well as unbelievable numerical growth. At times, the church has ruled the world and enjoyed seemingly unlimited power. Revivals have come to some nations with such power and with such popular acceptance as to almost convert the entire population, and yet today the world is not converted. We are told that more people live in the world today than all who have lived from Adam to now. The world today is not a Christian world. Though some lands today are enjoying great spiritual growth and Christianity is on the increase, in other nations Christianity is on the decline. In the western world, Europe, and America, we are seeing a decline in Christian values.

> We enjoy benefits that Christians from history did not enjoy.

We enjoy benefits that Christians from history did not enjoy. We are better prepared to evangelize the world. We have the written Word on a scale never before attained. The Bible has been translated into more languages; we have modern media; we have institutions of learning, and our churches are, at least in America, enjoying prosperity. Travel is no longer a problem. Today one can reach almost any country in the world in twenty-four hours. Not only is travel faster, but it is also safer.

We have almost two thousand years of church history behind us. We can evaluate the successes and the mistakes of the centuries gone by. We can see where separatism hindered church growth. The light of the Gospel was hidden. We also can see the ravages of secularism and how it has dimmed the light of the Gospel and caused the salt to lose its savor.

The walls that we have built give very little protection to the church and hinder immensely the church's outreach to the world.

The key today is involvement. We must be involved with our world. In light of the history of Christianity, we understand why some people today are afraid to get involved. It seems that every renewal or awakening in the church has ended with the church becoming lukewarm and unconcerned. Many feel that getting involved outside of the church family is to court disaster. In the last fifty years, pastors of some congregations have taught a strict separation from the world. As a result, many Christians have no contact with it. The walls that we have built give very little protection to the church and hinder immensely the church's outreach to the world. The Christian thrives on spiritual warfare. As we walk with God and fight the battle that He has put before us, we grow spiritually stronger. When the Christian retreats from the battle and separates himself from the world, he becomes spiritually weak.

Several years ago, a man in England inherited an estate in Scotland. When he had an opportunity, he traveled to see his inheritance and was surprised to find that it consisted of a beautiful old castle in a state of partial disrepair. Villagers from the nearby village had been coming to the castle and removing stones for the purpose of repairing their homes. Afraid of further damage to the castle, the owner hired a contractor to build a fence around the castle to protect it. After several years, the owner returned once again to see the castle, with the intention of repairing it as a home for retirement. Upon nearing the estate, he was astonished to see a huge stone wall surrounding the estate and the castle completely gone. Upon questioning the contractor as to the whereabouts of the castle, the owner received this answer: "I thought it would be a pity to buy material for a fence when all that stone was just going to waste, so I used the stones to build the fence." This is a fairly good example of what happens to the Christian that builds walls to protect himself from the world. After a while, there is nothing to protect and also the world has received no benefit from our existence. John Stott in *Involvement, Vol. 1*, said:

> It is exceedingly strange that any followers of Jesus Christ should ever have needed to ask whether social involvement was their concern, and that controversy should have blown up over the relationship between evangelism and social responsibility. For it is evident that in His public ministry Jesus both 'went about...teaching...and

preaching' (Matthew 4:35 RSV) and 'went about doing good and healing' (Acts 10:38 RSV).[17]

The ministry of Jesus included both a proclamation of hope, and social involvement with the people. He graces a wedding in Cana of Galilee with His presence. (See John 2:1-11.) He was accused of being gluttonous and consorting with drunkards and winebibbers. (See Matthew 11:19.) He attended a dinner at the house of a Pharisee and ministered to publicans and sinners to the consternation of the Pharisees and scribes. (See Luke 14:1; 15:1.)

Nathaniel Pugh, in *Living in the Tower*, said:

Jesus did not spend much time in the synagogues. He went to where the people were and mixed easily among them. Where did He go to preach His keynote sermon? He went to the side of a mountain with a rock for His pulpit.[18]

If we are to emulate the life of Christ, it is imperative that we get involved!

One problem we face with presenting the Gospel to the world is we are not sure that it is sufficient in itself. If we have rejected the separatist idea, then immediately we are tempted to dress up the Gospel to make it attractive to unbelievers. The Bible speaks of the last days when there would be men who, having a form of godliness, would deny the power thereof. (See 2 Timothy 3:5.) Paul instructed Timothy to turn away from such men. These are those that profess a knowledge of God but have no actual faith in Him. John Fischer in *Real Christians Don't Dance*, said:

> The success of the Gospel in our present age does not depend on how attractively it is packaged, but on how honestly real Christians are living out their lives in the world. That's a message you simply cannot dress up, especially if you tell the whole truth about yourself.
>
> We don't use deception. We won't draw people into a net and then surprise them with the Gospel. We set forth the Gospel plainly through words of truth and words of honesty from our lives. We trust God, the Great Designer, to handle His own image.[19]

One of the problems of our age is that we have experts in the art of dressing up the Gospel. Certain T.V. evangelists have been commercially successful at dressing up the Gospel. However, it appears that their own lives have caused them to have a very negative effect on our society. What we need are specialists in the art of living, not experts in the art of packaging!

It is obvious that it is easier to stray into a secular or worldly life style or slip into a separatist attitude, than to live by faith in this world. Samuel H. Miller, in *Man the Believer*, discusses the importance and the difficulty of living for God in this age of unbelief. Miller believes that we must go out and live in this world. Miller says,

You cannot discover your self without discovering what this world is. The depth and dark duplicity of it, the torment of its magnitude, the subterranean cellars and the Himalayan heights—all these things are both outside of history and the inside of humanity. You belong to it as surely as Adam or Ulysses or Oedipus belonged; without it you will not know yourself. And finally, without yourself and the world, the question of God can scarcely be raised. This is the greatest risk of all, the final limit, the farthest frontier where the great gamble is made—either God or nothing.[20]

Knowing what Miller is talking about would keep an individual from ever advocating a secular or social gospel. A separatist experience would keep you from knowing what he is talking about.

When the lives of Christians so closely parallel the lives of unbelievers, the Christian witness suffers. The drastic changes in the morality of the western world are due undoubtedly to many things. However, John Stott, in the book *Involvement: Social and Sexual Relationships in the Modern World*, says the greatest single reason for the higher divorce rate in the west is due to "the decline of Christian faith ... together with the loss of commitment to a Christian understanding of the sanctity and permanence of marriage."[21] Obviously this is a sign that secularism has done its job well. The fact that Christian behavior is following the trend of the world is in itself proof of a change in, or lack of understanding in Christian beliefs. R. C. Sproul, in *Ethics and the Christian World,* said,

> Obviously there must be a relationship between our ethical theories and our moral behavior. In a real sense our beliefs dictate our behavior. A theory underlies our every moral action. We may not be able to articulate that theory or even be immediately conscious of it, but nothing manifests our value systems more sharply than our actions.[22]

If the decline in morals and ethics were related only to unbelievers, then the light of the gospel would shine brighter and continue to do its work. The Scripture assures us, "When the enemy shall come in like a flood, the spirit of the Lord shall lift up a standard against him" (Isaiah 59:19). And "...where sin abounded, grace did much more abound" (Romans 5:20). The Christian does not have to fear the darkness of the world, for God has designed His church to be victorious in every situation. The Christian life is like a boat. Boats are designed to be put in the water. Christians are designed to live in the world. Problems arise when you put water in the boat, or the world in a Christian. Separatists won't put their boat in the water, and a secularist or social Christian won't take the water out of his boat.

We must always remember that God is in control of His church. It is impossible for us to understand why the wind blows in the direction that it does, but we must understand that God knows. God uses the excesses of man to bring about interest in Him and in His ways. Lewis B. Smedes, in *Mere Morality*, offers hope for the condition of our society with these words:

> To people cut off from any moral or spiritual tradition, perhaps hankering for something to help them keep their balance on the slippery shingles of freedom, any claim to represent what God expects us to do may evoke recollections of a childhood faith forever lost. Still, freedom without direction and responsibility without rules get to be burdensome after awhile, and we may be more ready than we have been for awhile to ask whether there is a way to get to know the will of God.[23]

Now is the time to live what the Bible teaches, not with a legalistic outlook, but because God has provided salvation for us. What worked for the first church will work for the church today.

J. Herbert Kane said in *Wanted: World Christians*,

> Well, God is not dead. He is very much alive. Moreover, He is still in control of the world and has not abandoned His plan one day to redeem the

world. To this end He is actively at work in the worldwide missionary movement of our day.

We can be thankful that, in spite of the moral decadence in our country, God has not forsaken us. He is quietly going about the task of renewing His church. Church membership in the United States now stands at about 63 percent of the population—an all-time high.[24]

We, as believers, must live in faith knowing that "what He had promised, He was able also to perform" (Romans 4:21). Others watch our lives, and we must have faith in our hearts, as well as Christian ethics and principles, if we are to be successful witnesses.

David J. Hesselgrave spoke of the care we should use in evangelizing unbelievers. He mentioned a time in Indonesia when people walked for miles to hear the gospel, and certain missionary workers hindered the work because they were more interested in taking pictures than in the actual salvation of souls. Hesselgrave described it,

> The people are ready to listen to Christian witnesses who understand and love them. But missionary opportunists who simply preach, take pictures, and write articles for publications in the West will do more harm than good. We need, not just more missionaries, but more missionaries who are men and women of God and who understand how to communicate Christ in our culture.[25]

Juan Carlos Ortiz, in *Call to Discipleship*, mentions three areas that hinder the Christian's involvement in our world: first, the eternal childhood of the believer. Ortiz thinks that we fail to disciple the converts in our churches, and they never grow up spiritually. It does seem that much time is spent accumulating numbers, pacifying them, and then accumulating more numbers. Ortiz quoted a new convert who, after six months in the church, said he had learned and knew as much as anyone in the church. Second is the misplacement of the believers. Ortiz says that many people never find their place in the body of Christ. Third is the lack of unity.[26]

Ortiz has given us three keys to reaching this generation: discipleship, helping others to find their place in the church, and the much talked about, but seldom practiced, art of loving one another as Christ loved us.

Conclusion

God's church is a victorious church. He has, through His mercy, placed us in His church. Our performance depends not on our abilities or opportunities, but on how we yield to the influence of God in our lives. It is our desire to be of service in the work of God. We know that to be successful or unsuccessful in the eyes of our associates is unimportant. The important thing is to be faithful.

To separate ourselves from our society is unfruitful. God places us in society to let our light shine and to bring hope to those in darkness. To separate ourselves from society is counter-productive. It will hinder our own spiritual growth and, as history has shown, bring about the very things we had tried to shun. Separation from evil is not the same as separation from society. We are instructed in God's Word to shun evil, even the appearance of evil. God, however, placed us in this world as salt to add flavor. He also reminded the apostles that they were not of this world. Though we are in the world, we are not of the world.

Some feel it will be easier to attract the unbeliever if we can prove to them that we, as Christians, are not so very different from them. One man bragged that he had worked for five years at a certain factory and no one even knew he was a Christian. The danger of the social or secular church is that it loses the very ingredient, godliness, which is able to make it a success.

> **The danger of the social or secular church is that it loses the very ingredient, godliness, which is able to make it a success.**

Perhaps the best way to explain the Christian's position in society is the example of the missionary working in a different culture. He must socialize and mix with the people of his chosen mission field; however, he may not participate in their pagan ideals. He must learn to love them, to enjoy their food and their way of life, but never do anything to cause them to lose respect for him as an emissary of God. In like manner, the Christian must live in this world, love the people, eat their food, respect and love their way of life, but never act in any way to cause them to question his loyalty and allegiance to his God.

Jesus became the perfect example of this when He came from heaven, was born of a woman, suffered and lived in this world. He lived with mankind, loved them, and died, all that we might be saved. He did not separate Himself from us, nor did He join us in our sin, but lived the perfect example before us.

---

[1] R. E. O. White, "Sanctification," in *Evangelical Dictionary of Theology*, ed. Walter A. Elwell (Grand Rapids: Baker Book House, 1984), 971.

[2] William L. Coleman, *The Pharisee's Guide to Total Holiness* (Minneapolis: Bethany House Publishers, 1977), 6-7.

[3] C. T. Marshall, "Monasticism," in *Evangelical Dictionary of Theology*, ed. Walter A. Elwell (Grand Rapids: Baker Book House, 1984), 728.

[4] M. A. Noll, "Pietism," in *Evangelical Dictionary of Theology*, ed. Walter A. Elwell (Grand Rapids: Baker Book House, 1984), 855-856.

[5] Ibid.

[6] Harold L. Bussell, *Lord, I Can Resist Anything But Temptation* (Grand Rapids: Zondervan, 1985), 167-170.

[7] Klaus Bockmuehl, "Secularization and Secularism: Some Christians Considerations." *Evangelical Review of Theology* (January 1986), 54-55.

[8] Ibid., 57.

[9] Jacques Ellul, *The Subversion of Christianity* (Grand Rapids: Eerdmans, 1986), 3.

[10] Theodore H. Epp, *Living Abundantly*, Vol.1 (Lincoln: Back to the Bible Broadcast, 1973), 19.

[11] J. Herbert Kane, *A Concise History of the Christian World Mission* (Grand Rapids: Baker, 1985), 7.

[12] Ibid., 17.

[13] Ibid.

[14] Ibid., 18.

[15] Ibid., 20.

[16] Ibid., 21.

[17] John Stott, *Involvement: Being a Responsible Christian in a Non-Christian Society* (Old Tappan: Revell, 1985), 19.

[18] Nathaniel Pugh, *Living in the Tower* (Hazelwood: Word Aflame, 1986), 34.

[19] John Fischer, *Real Christians Don't Dance* (Minneapolis: Bethany House Publishers, 1988), 23.

[20] Samuel H. Miller, *Man the Believer* (New York: Abingdon Press, 1968), 61.

[21] John Stott, *Involvement: Social and Sexual Relationships in the Modern World*, vol.2, (Old Tappan: Revell, 1985), 159.

[22] R. C. Sproul, *Ethics and the Christian* (Wheaton: Tyndale, 1989), 11.

[23] Lewis B. Smedes, *Mere Morality* (Grand Rapids: Eerdmans, 1989), 1.

[24] J. Herbert Kane, *Wanted: World Christians* (Grand Rapids: Baker, 1988), 17.

[25] David J. Hesselgrave, *Communicating Christ Cross-Culturally* (Grand Rapids: Zondervan, 1978), 460.

[26] Juan Carlos Ortiz, *Call to Discipleship* (Plainfield: Logos, 1975), 4-8, 26-28, 115-134.

Chapter 7

Viability of Integrating Psychology and Oneness Pentecostal Theology

By Mark A. Segraves

Mark A. Segraves, B.A., M.A., Ph.D. (Cand.)

The Director of the Department of Distance Learning, Mark Segraves earned the Bachelor of Arts degree from *Christian Life College* in 1991 and immediately began his ministry as a full-time evangelist. In 1992 he was licensed by the *United Pentecostal Church International*. Segraves has served in a variety of ministries, including Director of Promotions and show host for KCJH radio, field representative for *Tupelo Children's Mansion,* a teacher at Stockton Christian School, assistant pastor, youth pastor, and pastor.

He attended *San Joaquin Delta College* and *Covenant Theological Seminary* before earning the Master of Arts degree in Marriage, Family and Child Counseling from *Western Seminary* in 1999. He is currently a candidate for the Ph.D. in General Psychology from *Capella University*. In addition to his teaching and administrative duties at *Christian Life College,* Brother Segraves serves as an Adjunct Professor for the *Urshan Graduate School of Theology.* Mark and his wife, Robin Renee Segraves, have two children, Luke and Christiana.

Viability of Integrating Psychology and Oneness Pentecostal Theology

By Mark A. Segraves

Introduction

During the last one hundred years, the church has experienced exponential growth in tandem with a return to first century doctrine and practice. This includes, but is not limited to, the necessity of repentance, baptism by immersion in the name of Jesus Christ, the infilling of the Holy Spirit with the evidence of speaking in other tongues, the importance of living a separated life, the belief that God still performs miracles, and that the gifts of the Spirit are for the church today.

Around the world, contemporary testimonies of the miraculous power of God are common. People suffering with incurable diseases have been healed. Blind eyes have been given sight. Deaf ears have been opened. Even death has demonstrated its inadequacy in the face of the power of God as the dead have been brought back to life. Perhaps now more than ever, believers are looking at impossible obstacles through eyes of faith, and the miracles that result are almost too numerous to count.

At times, however, believers exercise their faith, proclaim the power of God, and speak the word of deliverance only to stand in perplexity waiting for a miracle that never comes. If the faith of the believer is fueled only by a perpetual demonstration of the power of God, the believer may experience a sense of doubt or a loss of hope. A person of stronger faith may survive the questions and relegate the absence of the miracle to the sovereign and unknowable will of God. In either case, the person in need remains in need.

Such a person is frequently directed to wait on God, to trust in God, and to continue to serve the Lord faithfully through the application of spiritual disciplines (e.g., prayer, fasting, Bible-reading, church attendance, giving, etc.). Clichés are often offered, such as: "It will happen in God's good time" or "Just hold on to the horns of the altar until God gives you what you need." Tragically, some believers interpret unanswered prayer as evidence that faith is somehow insufficient or hidden sin exists. Like Job, the person in need ends up in a vicious cycle of shame and guilt as he or she attempts to discern the motivation for God's silence. A question naturally grows out of such a situation: How does a believer cope when God seems silent?

Another question, perhaps even more baffling and painful than the first, reflects the reality of the fallen world around us and the influence of the fallen nature on even the most devout believer. Perhaps the question is better understood if described, rather than stated. A Christian couple divorces. A Christian teenager overdoses. A pastor commits adultery. A Christian man, married for eight years, confesses to a secret lifestyle of homosexuality. A pastor's wife is hospitalized with symptoms of what the psychiatrist calls a mental illness. These true-to-life scenarios are only a small sample of the many that could be offered here—tragic descriptions of heart-breaking scripts played out by wounded actors.

Similar to the first question, some believers respond to these scenarios with questions about the quality of faith in the lives of the fallen or the presence of sin in those victimized by the sinful choices of others. Like the disciples, these believers wonder who sinned in an effort to determine the cause of such harsh "punishment." In the meantime, the hurting—whether the offended or the offender—are often left without answers, support, or hope. When someone does offer help, it may only be the regurgitation of trivial maxims or, at worst, the reenactment of a comforter of Job. Again, the question naturally arises: How does a believer cope when nothing seems to work?

Many sincere Christians in these situations have applied every Scriptural principle they can think of and prayed every prayer their wounded spirit can utter. But the divorce goes through. The overdosed teenager dies. The pastor is not restored and loses church and family. The homosexual man comes out of the closet and walks out of the house never to be heard from again. The pastor's wife is consigned to a long-lasting regimen of psychotropic medication.

In an effort to provide sufficient support and effective ministry, some pastors have offered these hurting people pastoral counseling or referred them to qualified Christian counselors or psychologists. In cases where no Christian counselor or psychologist is available, some pastors have suggested utilizing counselors or psychologists who may be of a different religious persuasion or have no religious faith at all. Other pastors have felt that utilizing professional counseling or psychological resources—whether the professional is a Christian or not—is in direct opposition to the principles of Scripture. In this case, the pastor may continue to encourage the application of scriptural principles and the faithful practice of spiritual disciplines or, with no further recourse available, give up hope of seeing positive change.

Some pastors and believers—seeing the continuance of negative symptoms and the futility of giving up hope—have made an effort to develop a "biblical" approach to counseling, hoping to avoid any connection to the field of secular counseling and psychology. From a different perspective, some religious denominations have begun to wrestle with the perceived tension between psychology and theology. As a result, scholars—psychologists and theologians—have attempted to formulate an integration of the two.

A Tale of Two Perspectives

Before a discussion concerning the viability of integrating psychology and theology is possible, it is helpful to look at some historical issues. Hundreds of years before Christianity became a dominant force in the world, men like Zarathustra (Zoroaster), Siddhartha Gautama (Buddha), and Confucius wrestled with concepts like the mind, the soul, and behavior.[1] The conclusions drawn were not wholeheartedly accepted, but they did provide a makeshift foundation for the embryonic psychology that developed in ancient Greece. Because these men were religious in some form (e.g., Zoroaster was a priest, worshippers of Buddha meet in temples, contemporary believers in the philosophies of Confucius meet in "churches," etc.), it is not surprising that the philosophies they developed were affected to some extent by their faith or religion. In fact, one of the most consistent things observed across the spectrum of human existence is the creation of or worship of some kind of higher power. Brennan refers to the Egyptian supermarket of gods, where you had a choice of higher powers from the sun to house cats.[2]

Into this mix came the philosophers of ancient Greece, with their varying orientations toward psychological activity (e.g., naturalistic, biological, mathematical, eclectic, humanistic, etc.). When Christianity, mainly in the form of the Roman Catholic

Church, became a force to be reckoned with in the early centuries of historical Christianity, these orientations were deemed unfit for a church constructed on the premise of faith. In order to make the transition from philosophy to religion more effective, the church began to incorporate those components of philosophy that could fit within the framework of its dogmas. Brennan gives a good example of this when he shows how the Hebrew doctrine of monotheism (the belief in one God) may have been intermingled with the Greek tradition of polytheism (the belief in many gods) and resulted in the concept of the trinity (the belief that one God exists in three persons).[3]

For many years, the Papacy maintained an overwhelming sense of power and control over its members, which represented a major segment of society. This power was sufficient until men started asking the philosophical questions that had interested them for centuries. When this happened, the power of the Papacy declined and the quest for scientific thought revived. To stifle this movement, a series of crusades was launched in an attempt to restore power to the Papacy. The result, however, was the exact antithesis. Through the influence of Muslim scholars, who had preserved the writings and philosophies of the ancients, the Christian world was shaken and the power of the Papacy was never the same.

The influential Augustine attempted to promote his philosophy of the evils of the body and its senses, but Thomas Aquinas later resurrected the naturalistic and biological orientations as he showed the validity of using sensory experiences coupled with intellectual knowledge as the basis for the search for truth.[4] Aquinas, a theologian of the church, introduced these concepts of elementary psychological thought into faith-based religion, and his work forms the basis for the philosophical direction the study of psychology has taken since that time.

The ancient conflict between theology and philosophy, and its offspring, psychology, has continued in more recent years. It is mirrored in the friction that exists between religion and science. For example, Sigmund Freud said, "Of the three powers which may dispute the basic position of science, religion alone is to be taken seriously as an enemy."[5] Because of positions like this, some psychotherapists or psychoanalysts have chosen to ignore or at least minimize the concept of spirituality or religious experience as it impacts the lives of their clients. However, in more recent years, the discussion has been resurrected as a valid and even necessary issue. The concept of integrating spirituality, religion or theology with psychology has become so prominent a concern to many psychotherapists, that the American Psychological Association has published a variety of books related to spirituality, counseling, and psychotherapy.[6]

The substantive lack of integrative studies during past centuries is an indication of the result of an ancient line being drawn in the sand of philosophy. On one side stands the church, demanding that its religious mores, doctrines, and experiences be accepted and practiced by faith alone. On the other stands science, with its demand for strict adherence to principles of scientific observation as the basis for the acquisition of knowledge. This face-off has produced radical conclusions on both sides of the line. Some Christian believers have attempted to sever any form of secular counseling and psychology from spirituality or religious experience.[7] Freud's opinion of religion in relationship to science—specifically, psychology—has already been cited.[8]

The effect of the demands of the Papacy upon its constituents to adhere to a system of regulations and behaviors by faith alone is still felt throughout Christendom. Members of churches feel a tremendous sense of guilt and shame if they find themselves seeking scientific proof for something previously accepted by faith alone. This dilemma brings us to an issue worth wrestling with. Just as Aristotle and Thomas Aquinas attempted to move people from the positions postulated by Plato and Augustine, we too have a task: to develop a more complete science of psychology without contradicting Scripture, while we attempt, at the same time, to respect and even understand the framework of faith and religious experience many parishioners bring to the table.[9]

The Perilous Journey

Even though the power of the organized church had been reduced in many areas by the seventeenth century, it still maintained control over certain parts of society, specifically, southern Europe.[10] An evidence of that control could be seen in the universities, where scientific exploration and reformulation were controlled by either the church or the government. Because of factors like this, independent societies of scholars were created for the purpose of advancing scientific knowledge. When the existing government threatened the emerging freedom of scientific inquiry, the societies were there to promote such freedom. When the universities were slow to move toward the development of new scientific knowledge because of the power of theological faculty members, or the university's conservative policies, the societies were there to push the boundaries and explore new territory.[11]

The two major traits consistent within all learned societies was their desire for freedom from influence by the church and government and their passion of developing new scientific knowledge in the face of the sometimes lackadaisical scholarship found in the universities.[12]

The Scholarly Societies Project reports that "from their earliest beginnings, scholarly societies played a major role in bringing scholars together in meetings where they could discuss and exchange ideas."[13] This forum, created by the advent of the societies, produced an environment conducive to the development of scientific thought and, at the same time, began to lay the foundation for a standard of quality to be achieved. Even though the universities of the seventeenth century had many dynamic scholars, the societies were responsible for the majority of scholarly journals to be written during the period.[14]

These learned societies provide the foundation for current organizations like the American Psychological Association. In fact, while separated by more than three hundred years, there are still many similarities. The purpose of the current societies (e.g., APA, APS, etc.) is to promote the advancement of scientific thought, while providing a scholarly standard to which all contributors must adhere. Unlike the early societies, the APA and other groups have academic freedom to explore and develop ideas under the watchful eye of their leaders and constituency, within the less-restricting parameters of local government. Nonetheless, in some ways the church still maintains—and rightfully so—a careful attitude about anything that may contradict sound doctrine or minimize the importance of faith. Some in the church feel like science stands in opposition to faith or religion. Likewise, some in the church feel like psychology stands in opposition to theology. However, there are a growing number of Christian scholars, pastors, and lay people—this author included—who disagree with these absolute statements.

Theology and Psychology: Is Integration Possible?

My background includes a B.A. in Bible and Theology from Christian Life College, an institution endorsed by the United Pentecostal Church International. After briefly attending Covenant Theological Seminary (St. Louis, MO), I earned the Master of Arts in Marriage and Family Therapy through Western Seminary (Portland, OR/San Jose, CA). This particular degree required a substantial number of courses in theology. I am currently completing the dissertation for the Ph.D. in general psychology from Capella University (Minneapolis, MN). My purpose in describing this history is not intended to be self-aggrandizing. Rather, it is intended to add meaning to the various reactions I have encountered during the past few years. For example, while communicating with a licensed minister about my decision to enter the Ph.D. program, I was told that I was on the "devil's pathway" and that I would lose my ministry and eventually walk away from God. Another licensed minister—a person I had never met or conversed with—conveyed to one of my close friends that he considered me to be a reprobate because of my decision. I found all of this interesting, because the statements were not based on any personal knowledge of my spiritual condition. On the other hand, other licensed ministers have expressed to me their appreciation and relief that someone was actually pursuing formal training in this area because the needs of the people they ministered to seem so overwhelming. Like some other denominations or organizations, Oneness Pentecostals are just beginning to wrestle with these concepts. The primary question remains unanswered. Can Oneness theology interface with psychology with the result of biblically-sound integration?

Different models of integration have been proposed by various Christian scholars (e.g., Crabb, Minirth, Meier, Narramore, etc.), and a few of the models have merit. One of the most important concepts in any discussion of integration is that all truth is God's truth. This simply means that some things not found in Scripture are true. One of the most oft-cited examples is a mathematical problem. 2 + 2 = 4. This statement is not found in Scripture, but it is still true and, by extension, does not contradict the Word of God.

To truly grasp this concept, it is necessary to understand the difference between general and special revelation. General revelation refers to God's disclosure of

Himself through the created universe (e.g., Psalm 19:1-3). When God does something outside of the laws of nature in order to reveal Himself, we call it special revelation (e.g., written Scripture, the Incarnation, etc.). The Bible is a special revelation with an intended purpose – to convey the message of the grand drama of redemption and to lead us to Christ.

At the same time, the Bible does not address certain issues (e.g., is it right or wrong to utilize psychotropic medication to alleviate negative symptoms like hallucinations?). Over the last couple of centuries scientific discoveries have led to cures for various diseases, medical procedures that lengthen life and promote healthy living, and the alleviation of certain levels of pain. Whether the scientist acknowledges God as the source or not, these discoveries are based on principles or laws God instilled in the created world. Many Christians have no problem utilizing medical science to lengthen life or to alleviate pain, but this attitude is not always the same in relation to psychological theory and practice.

In spite of this, some Oneness Pentecostals—including myself—are interested in developing a biblically-sound model of integration. In the future, I will attempt to present a more thorough discussion related to integration, but for now, let me share with you several concepts I believe will be necessary if such a model is ever to be accepted in Oneness Pentecostal circles.

First, psychological *theory* must not contradict Scripture. If the theoretical underpinnings of a psychological school of thought contradict Scripture, the theory must be altered. If no viable alteration is possible, the theory must be discarded.

Second, psychological *practice* must not contradict Scripture. Where theory provides a reason, practice provides a method. Any method utilized in treating or helping hurting people must be consistent with Scripture.

Third, human beings must be looked at holistically. It is not enough to view a human being as a soul. Man is more than a soul. Even the Apostle Paul saw the importance of wholeness in every facet of human existence (1 Thessalonians 5:23).

> Man is more than a soul.

Fourth, integration must not be a "Christianizing" of secular psychology. For example, taking Freud's theory of personality (the id, the ego, and the superego) and equating it to the Christian concepts of the sinful nature, the indwelling Holy Spirit, and the conscience is overly simplistic and reductionistic.

These four concepts are elementary building blocks in the monumental challenge of developing an integrative model, but it is a challenge I believe Oneness Pentecostalism is ready to face. My sincere hope is that any attempt at integration will be built on a foundation of much prayer, faithfulness to the Word of God, and a quality of scholarly inquiry that brings glory to God.

[1] James F. Brennan, *Readings in the History and Systems of Psychology* (Upper Saddle River, NJ: Prentice Hall, 1998).

[2] Ibid.

[3] Ibid.

[4] James F. Brennan, *Readings in the History and Systems of Psychology* (Upper Saddle River, NJ: Prentice Hall, 1998b).

[5] Sigmund Freud, *New Introductory Lectures on Psychoanalysis* (New York: W.W. Norton & Company, 1933/1965).

[6] P. Scott Richards and Allen E. Bergin, *A Spiritual Strategy for Counseling and Psychotherapy* (Washington, DC: American Psychological Association, 1997).

[7] Jay E. Adams, *Competent to Counsel* (Grand Rapids, MI: Zondervan Publishing House, 1986).

[8] Freud, 1933/1965.

[9] Brennan, 1998.

[10] Ibid.

[11] Ibid.

[12] Ibid.

[13] Jim Parrott, ed., *Scholarly Societies Project* (published 2000, amended 2004), online; accessed June 23, 2004; available from http://www.scholarly-societies.org/editorial_20000327.html.

[14] Ibid.

Chapter 8

Spiritual Disciplines in a Postmodern Culture

By Lonnie Vestal

Lonnie Vestal, B.A.

A native of Statesville, North Carolina, Lonnie Vestal attended *Christian Life College* where he earned the Bachelor of Arts degree in Bible and Theology in 2000. He returned to *Christian Life College* in 2001 as an instructor and fills various other roles on campus. He met and married his wife, Jill, during his college years. He is currently pursuing a Master's Degree in Exegetical Theology at *Western Seminary,* San Jose.

Spiritual Disciplines in a Postmodern Culture

By Lonnie Vestal

Introduction

One cannot reflect long upon the life of Jesus without considering the spiritual disciplines that marked his ministry. In fact, spiritual disciplines such as prayer and fasting were so a part of his life that we might understand them as self-applied "disciplines". In the case of Jesus they are perhaps best described in terms of the lifestyle itself, since they did not impose themselves upon an otherwise carnal nature. Likewise, what we know about the lifestyles of His disciples suggests they were no less committed to a life of spiritual discipline.[1] If Paul's ministry is indicative of the other disciples' ministries, we know that these disciplines, in addition to giving them spiritual strength, were the means by which they obtained direction (both literal and spiritual) for their ministries (Acts 16:6-7).[2]

However, when reflecting upon Christendom today, there seems to be a great disparity between the practices of the first-century church and those of the typical North American church. Thus, the question could be asked: are the spiritual disciplines headed for extinction? This question is particularly relevant to the Pentecostal movement, since it traces its roots to the humble mission at Azuza Street, Los Angeles. It was there that William Seymour, through much prayer and fasting, ushered in the greatest Pentecostal revival of the early 20th century.

Indeed, it seems that most if not all revivals have been preceded by a renewed emphasis on the spiritual disciplines. Those pastors who recognize the validity of spiritual disciplines seem to experience numerical growth more consistently, which is, in reality, a reflection of the spiritual growth brought about through their spiritual disciplines. John Wesley, founder of the early Methodist movement, which in its inception had more similarities than differences to the modern Pentecostal movement, was one such pastor. When asked about the potential longevity of the Methodist movement, he responded by saying,

> The Methodists must take heed to their doctrine, their experience, their practice, and their discipline. If they attend to their doctrines only, they will make the people antinomians; if to the experimental part of religion only, they will make them enthusiasts; if to the practical part only, they will make them Pharisees; and if they do not attend to their discipline, they will be like persons who bestow much pains in cultivating their garden, and put no fence round it, to save it from the wild boar of the forest.[3]

John Wesley's insightful observation especially bears repetition following the recent decision made by the United Methodist Church (UMC) to allow Karen Dammann, a lesbian minister who was on trial for violating the UMC's Book of Discipline (particularly the part forbidding homosexual ministers), to continue practicing her homosexual lifestyle, thereby condoning the practice for all Methodist homosexual ministers. The immorality of the UMC's decision is surpassed only by the absurdity of the trial that forced judgment on the matter. One witness for the defense, Dammann's District Superintendent Ron Hines, claimed that Dammann had done much good in her pastorate and had "helped them reclaim what it means to be a church."[4]

This failed attempt to judge rightly is indicative of the lack of spiritual intimacy evidenced in the greater Christian community. Also, the decision of the UMC is telling of the nature of the problem: it is not an issue of spiritual stagnancy; it is one of fatal spiritual regression. The absence of the spiritual disciplines cannot be overlooked as one seeks to understand the journey from Wesley's dedication to his successors' apostasy and the reasons for such spiritual deterioration.

Although the Pentecostal movement, particularly the United Pentecostal Church International (UPCI), may never debate whether or not homosexuals can hold a ministerial license, there are other pertinent issues that threaten its existence and unity. Many issues are of such weight that they require judgment rich with the wisdom that comes only through the spiritual disciplines. The role the spiritual disciplines play in the future of the church needs to be revisited if travesty and division are to be avoided.

It would be overly-simplistic to say that spiritual disciplines have fallen out of use due to complacency and apathy. What is important to note are the explanations that account for the reasons they have fallen out of use, especially if we conclude that the present regression is *not* due to a failure on the previous generation's part to communicate their necessity. One explanation that *does* seem valid has to do with the postmodernist philosophical movement that has pervaded North American society. This philosophy, and the worldview it purports, was not nearly the obstacle to the Pentecostal movement in the early 20th century that it has become in the last thirty years. In fact, one might conclude that its predecessor, the modernist worldview, was actually conducive to the Pentecostal growth. According to Dr. Chris Witcombe, proponents of the modernist worldview felt that,

> "Truth" discovered through reason would free people from the shackles of corrupt institutions such as the Church .... The belief was that "the

truth shall set you free." ... Through truth and freedom, the world would be made into a better place.[5]

Modernists of the early 20th century who acknowledged the existence of objective truth were more apt to receive the ultimate truth of the gospel. Conversely, those who are influenced by the postmodernist worldview will most likely either reject it out of hand or mentally relegate it to the same status of other world religions. Subsequently, the lifestyles, or spiritual disciplines, that flow from faith in Jesus become another casualty of postmodernist relativism. Therefore, this chapter will attempt to examine the philosophical shift that is identified as postmodernism and the ways in which the church can counteract its influence upon the saints, particularly as it relates to the much-needed spiritual disciplines that its Cornerstone exhibited.

The Postmodern Shift

The devolution of human thought has led to the postmodern age.[6] If postmodernism is a movement, then the philosophy that under-girds it is known as "deconstruction." There is little consensus—neither among its proponents nor among its detractors—as to what are the tenants of postmodern doctrine. Indeed, no one has produced a definitive work on postmodernism, a fact that should suggest its volatile and nihilistic nature. However, the one fundamental principle of the postmodernist is the denial of all foundational, *a priori* categories upon which man can base human reasoning.[7] The epistemological and theological ramifications are as follows: First, this leads to the conclusion that the epistemological base-superstructure (and/or narrow-based foundationalism) metaphor is invalid. This means essentially that "there is no direct experience of reality without interpretation; and all interpretation is in some sense corrupted by the cultural and personal prejudices or prejudgments of the interpreter."[8] Second, this leads to the conclusion that theology (and the lifestyle that it produces) is merely a subjective product, not applicable to any objective, rational paradigms of reality. To put it succinctly: truth is relative, and the authorities that claim to purport the truth may safely be disregarded.

Postmodernism then seeks to raze the base of things that can be known. The result is a society in which one's set of truth-claims does not necessarily have to correspond with objective reality (there is no such thing to a postmodernist); it merely has to correspond to his reality.

Obstacles Caused by Postmodern Thought

If absolute truth does not easily assimilate itself in a postmodern culture, then the outgrowth of that truth is all the more uncertain. This presents a true obstacle to applying the spiritual disciplines, because if truth is relative, how much more are the disciplines that result from the knowledge of that truth? To further frustrate matters, most theologians will admit that a correlation exists between the spiritual disciplines and spiritual maturity (a growing understanding of the truth), but how does one prove this to a postmodernist, especially when these same theologians will rightly agree that the spiritual disciplines are not "spiritual" in their mere performance; they are a means to an end? For example, at no point does performing the discipline of meditation produce anything. There is no objective, observable product that comes from the discipline itself; the ingredient of faith must be present if the discipline is to be beneficial to the individual. If there were a cause-effect relationship between what one did (performance of the disciplines) and what resulted from one's actions (spiritual maturity), then the value of the spiritual disciplines would be apparent to all. However, spiritual maturity is not mechanistic; it is relational. Therefore, theologians' attempts to correlate precisely the spiritual disciplines with spiritual maturity must begin by acknowledging this, and doing so will, in the mind of the postmodernist, make relative those things they seek to codify.

> Since a postmodernist does not recognize an objective basis for authority, then speaking as an authority is a doomed task.

The above obstacle mainly concerns the dilemma of codifying the spiritual disciplines. Another obstacle has to do with the person who seeks to codify them. Since a postmodernist does not recognize an objective basis for authority, then speaking as an authority is a doomed task. Indeed, authoritarianism has been replaced with a kind of "inner empiricism," where the "the source of authority... [is] nothing more than personal experience."[9] If this is true (which it is not), then the suggestion that one's experience is indicative of a necessary law is nothing less than an attempt to impose one's authority on the will of others. This assumption springs from the nihilistic notions of the postmodernist, which includes the belief that "there is no truth, no value, no concern. All that is left is 'The Will to Power'."[10] Traces of this mindset are evident even in Christian circles, so that pastors must now carefully couch the arguments for the spiritual disciplines in such a way that the saint is assured of the pastor's pure intentions.

Benefits of Postmodern Thought

In light of the obstacles mentioned, one might assume that postmodern thought can only hinder the application of spiritual disciplines. However, there are some aspects of postmodern thought that cohere with the disciplines. Emphasizing these aspects can help convince the reluctant believer to apply the disciplines and reap the benefits thereof.

An ironic benefit of postmodern thought is the rejection of empiricism and absolutism. On the one hand, truth, for the postmodernist, is relative, and thus any truth claims are subject to interpretation. While this mindset does not affirm truth, it does not deny it either, and the inability to completely deny the truth is for some a step forward. Furthermore, the rejection of empiricism of the Enlightenment reopens the door to the possibility of a supernatural world and experience.[11] In short, Christianity has once again become intellectually relevant.[12] In fact, postmodernists' reactionary tendencies against empiricism often mean that they welcome the supernatural experiences that can occur through a mastery of the spiritual disciplines.

Another benefit of the spiritual disciplines comes from the priority the postmodernist places on community. Individualism is shunned so much so that the postmodernist's belief system is derived solely from the community.[13] If the community both informs and motivates the postmodernist as to the content of his faith, then the spiritual disciplines will flourish in a Christian community if they are practiced and encouraged by enough members of that community. Dallas Willard discusses this opportunity by saying,

They welcome the supernatural experiences that can occur through a mastery of the spiritual disciplines.

> [The disciplines] are much more effective if they can be practiced in community, and you can't really practice them without community. If you have a community where they are understood as a normal part of our lives, there can be instruction or teaching about them, which brings about a kind of accountability.[14]

On the surface Willard's mention of accountability seems to destroy the spirit of the disciplines, since the disciplines should be done in response to the internal promptings of the Spirit. However, Willard is not advocating a coercive system of spiritual discipline enforcement, but rather he is encouraging an open dialogue in the community about the disciplines and the positive effects they have on the believers' relationship with God.

Conclusion

Ideally, the spiritual disciplines should not suffer or flourish as a result of newly emerging world views. They are, after all, something that the Spirit initiates for the purpose of bringing the believer into greater intimacy with Jesus and into more perfect conformity with the will of the Father. In theory, the believer should maintain the spiritual disciplines in the face of a sinful generation.

> The spiritual disciplines are not supplemental to a Christian walk of faith; they are very much necessary for the believer's faith to remain.

Humanly speaking, the spiritual disciplines are self-imposed mechanisms, subject to human misconceptions and neglect. The church, entrenched as it is in postmodern culture, can benefit from an understanding of the challenges and opportunities it faces as it presents the need for a renewal in the spiritual disciplines to a skeptical generation.

One thing seems amply evident from the witness of Scripture and history: the spiritual disciplines are not supplemental to a Christian walk of faith; they are very much necessary for the believer's faith to remain.

---

[1] See Acts 1:14; 3:1; 6:4; 12:5; Romans 12:12; 1 Corinthians 7:5; Ephesians 6:18; and Colossians 4:2.

[2] The Scripture simply says that the Spirit forbade Paul to go to Asia and Bythinia, but it is safe to say that prayer (or meditation) was the means by which he came to understand the Spirit's intentions.

[3] Rupert Davies, A. Raymond George, Gordon Rupp, eds. *A History of The Methodist Church in Great Britain, vol. 4* (London: Epworth Press, 1998), 194.

[4] Ron Hines, "testimony from Karen Dammann's trial," 17 Mar. 2004 [online posting]; accessed 30 Mar. 2004; available from http://www.umc.org/interior.asp?ptid=2&mid=3735.

[5] Dr. Chris L.C.E. Witcombe, "Modernism," originally in "What is Art?...What is an Artist?" 1997 available from http://witcombe.sbc.edu/modernism/roots.html.

[6] "Age" is an appropriate term to apply because, unlike the Industrial Revolution, which admittedly produced cultural and societal changes on a massive scale, postmodernism is a philosophical movement. Its penetration and pervasiveness promise to change human thought rather than mere human activity and lifestyle. This difference cannot be overlooked. On the one hand, the invention of power tools, the assembly line, etc., forced people to change things such as their occupation, their residence, and their standard of living. On the other hand, the doctrine of postmodernism changes the way people view life, reality, and faith. The latter is by far the more potent force. Furthermore, the infiltrative efforts of postmodernists have been so successful that countering and defeating this movement will take decades of consistent work. Therefore, it is still correct if not saddening to use the term "postmodern age."

[7] William Grassie, "Postmodernism: What One Needs to Know," *Zygon: Journal of Religion and Science* (March 1997): available from http://www.users.voicenet.com/~grassie/Fldr.Articles/Postmodernism.html.

[8] Grassie, n.p.
[9] Lee Campbell, Ph.D., "Postmodernism and You: Science," *The Crossroads Project* (1996): available from http://www.xenos.org/ministries/crossroads/dotsci.htm.
[10] D. Martin Fields, "Postmodernism," *Premise* 2, no. 8 (September, 1995): 5. Also published in Colin Brown, *Philosophy and the Christian Faith* (Downers Grove, IL: InterVarsity Press, 1968), 137-141.
[11] Fields, 5.
[12] Diogenes Allen, *Christian Faith in a Postmodern World: The Full Wealth of Conviction* (Louisville, KY: Westminster/John Knox, 1989), 5.
[13] Ironically, individualism is arguably the basis for moral relativism; this is just one of the internal inconsistencies to this worldview. See Stanley J. Grenz, *A Primer On Postmodernism* (Grand Rapids, MI: Wm. B. Eerdmans Publishing Co., 1996), 8.
[14] Dallas Willard, "A Conversation with Luci Shaw," *Radix* 27, No. 2.

Chapter 9

Contemplative Prayer
Lectio Divina: Readings in the Classics

By Robert H. Roam

Robert H. Roam, B.A.

Robert Roam attended *Gateway College of Evangelism* 1968-1970 and completed a Bachelor of Arts degree in Biblical Studies from *Christian Life College* in 2003. He was ordained with the *United Pentecostal Church International* in 1975. A native of St. Louis, Missouri, Roam attended his father's church where he received early ministerial training. He founded the church in Lynn, Massachusetts and served as pastor in Boise, Idaho, Farmington, Missouri, and Rupert, Idaho. He has served as district Youth President, and also as Home and Foreign Missions Directors.

Robert and Paula Roam joined the staff at *Christian Life College* in 1999 and directed the food service department. Robert Roam was promoted to Dean of Students in 2000 and also serves as the College Pastor. He is pursuing a Master of Arts degree in Leadership through *Hope International University*, Fullerton, California.

Contemplative Prayer
By Robert H. Roam

The art or practice of meditating on God and His Word goes back to the origin of man. Man was created with the ability to think and reason. When man and woman were first created in the Garden of Eden, God spoke to them. All throughout Scripture we see the benefits and blessings man received when he obeyed the words of God. We can also read about the judgment that comes to those who do not obey His words.

The children of Israel were to keep the Law given to them by God. Their whole lives were to be affected by the Word of God.

> Hear O Israel: The Lord our God is one Lord: And thou shalt love the Lord thy God with all thine heart, and with all thy soul, and with all thy might. And these words, which I command thee this day, shall be in thine heart: And thou shalt teach them diligently unto thy children, and shalt talk of them when thou sittest in thine house, and when thou walkest by the way, and when thou liest down, and when thou risest up. And thou shalt bind them for a sign upon thine hand, and they shall be as frontlets between thine eyes. And thou shalt write

them upon the posts of thy house, and on the gates (Deuteronomy 6:4-9).

When Moses died and Joshua became the leader of Israel the Lord spoke to him about keeping His Word. "This book of the law shall not depart out of thy mouth; but thou shalt meditate therein day and night, that thou mayest observe to do according to all that is written therein: for then thou shalt make thy way prosperous, and then thou shalt have good success" (Joshua 1:8). He was instructed to not only read the Word, but to also meditate on it day and night.

There are other references given in the Psalms about meditating upon the works, precepts, statutes, and the laws of God. The psalmist wrote,

Blessed is the man that walketh not in the counsel of the ungodly, nor standeth in the way of sinners, nor sitteth in the seat of the scournful. But his delight is in the law of the Lord; and in his law doth he *meditate* day and night (Psalm 1:1-2).

Another example is "Let the words of my mouth, and the meditation of my heart, be acceptable in thy sight, O Lord, my strength, and my redeemer" (Psalm 19:14).

The Apostle Paul wrote to Timothy,

Let no man despise thy youth; but be thou an example of the believers, in word, in conversation, in charity, in spirit, in faith, in purity. Till I come, give attendance to reading, to exhortation, to doctrine. Neglect not the gift that is in thee, which was given thee by prophecy, with the laying on of the hands of the presbytery. *Meditate* upon these things; give thyself wholly to them; that thy profiting may appear to all (1 Timothy 4:12-15).

Sacred Reading

Lectio Divina is a Latin expression which means sacred reading. It is "probably the most ancient form of mental prayer and the source of most other forms of quiet prayer. Jesus himself no doubt reflected on the words of the Scripture, especially the Psalms, in those quiet moments he spent in prayer."[1] The early church gathered together, "And they continued stedfastly in the apostles' doctrine and fellowship, and breaking of bread, and in prayers" (Acts 2:42).

Luke Dysinger in *Accepting the Embrace of God*, identified the specific process. He wrote,

> A very Ancient art, practiced at one time by all Christians, is the technique known as lectio divina – a slow, contemplative praying of the Scriptures which enables the Bible, the Word of God, to become a means of union with God. This ancient practice has been kept alive in the Christian monastic tradition, and is one of the precious treasures of Benedictine monastics and oblates.[2]

Lectio Divina differs from our usual style of reading. Michel de Verteuil, *Lectio Divina – Sacred Reading, A Method of Bible Reflection* explained the difference.

A bible text is not like a textbook or a newspaper, providing us with objective information. It was not written like that. Instead, it stirs up feelings; we find ourselves identifying with the characters, we feel for them, admire them or dislike them. We are caught up in the movement of the text, its suspense, its dramatic reversals of fortune, it unanswered questions.[3]

This type of reading to me is much deeper than other types of reading that I do. It is like savoring what is being read, not just tasting or sampling. Dysinger also pointed out the distinction between our normal method of reading and this *sacred reading* of the text.

The reading or listening which is the first step in *lectio divina* is very different from the speed reading which modern Christians apply to newspapers, books and even to the Bible. *Lectio* is reverential listening; listening both in a spirit of silence and of awe. We are listening for the still, small voice of God that will speak to us personally – not loudly, but intimately. In *lectio* we read slowly, attentively, gently listening to hear a word or phrase that is God's word for us this day.[4]

The weaknesses of *Lectio Divina* are much like any other form of prayer. Jesus warned,

And when thou prayest, thou shalt not be as the hypocrites are: for they love to pray standing in the synagogues and in the corners of the streets, that they may be seen of men. They have their reward. But thou, when thou prayest, enter into thy closet, and when thou hast shut thy door, pray to the Father which is in secret; and the Father which seeth in secret shall reward thee openly. But when ye pray, use not vain repetitions, as the heathen do: for they think that they shall be heard for their much speaking (Matthew 6: 5-7).

We must be sure our attitudes are right when we approach the Lord in prayer. It is necessary that *Lectio Divina* does not become a ritual that we do by going through the motions. There could also be a danger in individuals receiving their own personal revelations outside of the Word of God. "Knowing this first, that no prophecy of the scripture is of any private interpretation" (2 Peter 1:20).

> It is like savoring what is being read, not just tasting or sampling.

Another weakness could be an emphasis on works instead of grace. Some of the advocates of *Lectio Divino* in their writings seem to place a greater emphasis on what they do or don't do, instead of what Jesus does for us. I believe that Jesus wants us to be lights in this dark world, not sequestered some place away from society. We are to "Go ye therefore, and teach all nations..." (Matthew 28:19) We are to be His witnesses in all the world.

People need to see individuals whose lives have been changed by the power of the Gospel. We need to take the saving message to the masses, in the market place, in schools, at work, at play, and everywhere we go. Jesus teaches us that we are the salt of the earth, the light of the world, a city set on a hill, and that we are to let our lights shine before men that they may see our good works and glorify our Father which is in heaven (Matthew 5:13-16).

There are many more advantages than disadvantages to practicing *Lectio Divina*. Thomas Keating, in *The Classical Monastic Practice of Lectio Divina*, illustrated the benefits.

> *Lectio Divina* is a special kind of process, and to benefit fully from its fruits, its integrity has to be respected. The ripe fruit of the regular practice of *Lectio Divina* is assimilating the word of God and being assimilated by it. It is a movement from conversation to communion. It also enables us to express our deep spiritual experience of union with God in words or symbols that are appropriate. There is thus a movement not only into silence, but from silence to expression.[5]

Listening with the Heart

The form that is often used is to cultivate the ability to listen with our hearts to hear from the Lord or to allow Him to speak to us as we are reading the Word of God. "He that hath an ear, let him hear what the Spirit saith unto the churches...." (Revelation 2:7). In order to do this we must first begin to read in a slow discerning way, savoring each word or sentence we read. I know that personally there have been many times that as I was reading the Word of God, I would feel that the Lord was speaking to me from His Word.

There are many truths from the Scriptures that we have not gleaned as yet. There have been times that I received a fresh thought from a Scripture that I have read many times before. *Lectio Divina* allows us to be able to get much more from the Word as we read it in contemplation. In *Lectio Divina* we may read the same sentence or Scripture over and over, memorizing and allowing the Spirit of the Lord to speak to us from the Word.

> **Lectio Divina allows us to be able to get much more from the Word as we read it in contemplation.**

The next step is to pray. We allow the Word that we have just read to touch and change our lives. We can express to the Lord our hurts and problems while reciting the Word over and over applying his Word to our situations and also being changed by what we have read. We then rest in His presence as we contemplate His love for us. This is a wordless time that we simply sit in His presence, allowing ourselves to be refreshed by the Spirit. Again, first we select a Scripture and then become still as we read the Scripture slowly. We allow what we have read to interact with our thoughts, then speak to the Lord from our heart what we feel and then to finally rest in the presence of the Lord in a quiet manner.

Lectio Divina encourages one to take his time when reading and speaking to the Lord. Whereas many times we speak or read in a manner that is like skimming. *Lectio Divina* encourages us to listen to the voice within us that is often the voice of the Lord. Jeanne Guyon, in *Experiencing the Depths of Jesus Christ*, wrote, "What is attracting you so strongly to your inward parts? It is none other than God Himself. And, oh, His drawing of you causes you to run to Him."[6]

I cannot count the times that I have felt the drawing of the Spirit of the Lord to go deeper in Him. The yearning that is present is from the Lord Himself, although we do not always recognize who it is that is calling us. Jesus said,

> To him the porter openeth; and the sheep hear his voice: and he calleth his own sheep by name, and leadeth them out. And when he putteth forth his own sheep, he goeth before them, and the sheep follow him: for they know his voice. And a stranger will they not follow, but will flee from him: for they know not the voice of strangers (John 10:3-5).

Thomas Kelly, in *A Testament of Devotion,* said, "The Living Christ within us is the initiator and we are the responders."[7] This is where it is so important to be still and to listen for the "still small voice" that Elijah the Prophet spoke about in 1 Kings 19:12. This is sometimes easier said than done, as we are so easily distracted. How many times have we attempted to pray and suddenly all kinds of different thoughts enter our minds to distract us? We suddenly remember that we were supposed to call someone, or we forgot to do something else. I am finding that it takes an effort on my part to shut out the distractions and to focus on the voice of the Lord. However, it is like any other discipline, the more you do it the easier it becomes.

In the article, *"What do we mean by prayer?"* Evelyn Underhill stated, "Prayer, then, begins by an intellectual adjustment. By thinking of God earnestly and humbly to the exclusion of other objects of thought, by deliberately surrendering the mind to spiritual things, by preparing the consciousness for the inflow of new life."[8]

Even though I desire to listen to the voice of the Lord, I find myself repeating many prayers that I have prayed many times before. These prayers are important, but I have memorized them over the years and sometimes I can recite them without much thought. When I pray *Lectio Divina* style, I have to make myself concentrate much more on the request and carefully listen for the answer. Sometimes, even though I may not receive an immediate answer, I still feel the comfort of the presence of the Lord.

This is always gratifying, just knowing that I have felt him and been in His presence.

Experiencing His Presence

Lectio Divina is opening yourself up and exposing the secret chambers of the heart and inner thoughts to the Lord. Dallas Willard, in *The Divine Conspiracy,* stressed the importance of the *will* being surrendered to God.

> It is the *will* aspect of personal/spiritual realty that is its innermost core. In biblical language the will is usually referred to as "heart." This it is that organizes all the dimensions of personal reality to form a life or a person. The will, or heart, is the executive center of the self. Thus the center point of the spiritual in humans as well as in God is self-determination, also called freedom and creativity.[9]

It is not only being honest with God; it is being honest with yourself. It is pulling back the veneer and exposing the real you to the Lord. It is also acknowledging our need of the Lord's help. In the ancient classic, *The Imitation of Christ,* Thomas à Kempis wrote,

> The kingdom of God is peace and joy in the Holy Spirit, such as is not granted to wicked people. Our Lord Jesus Christ will come to you and will show you His consolations, if you will make ready for Him a dwelling place within. All that He desires in you is within yourself, and there it is His pleasure to be. There are between Almighty God and a devout soul many spiritual visitings, sweet inward

conversations, great gifts of grace, many consolations, much heavenly peace, and wondrous familiarity of the blessed presence of God.[10]

What a wonderful feeling of release it is to be able to confide in the Lord. I feel that this is really the starting point for restoration in every life. There is something about the presence of the Lord that illuminates our very being. This is the goal or aim of *Lectio Divina*, to be in the presence of the Lord.

In *Lectio Divina* there is much soul-searching. Thomas Merton, in *Contemplative Prayer*, said,

> In the *prayer of the heart* we seek first of all the deepest ground of our identity in God. We do not reason about dogmas of faith, or *the mysteries*. We seek rather to gain a direct existential grasp, a personal experience of the deepest truths of life and faith, *finding ourselves in God's truth*. Inner certainty depends on purification. The dark night rectifies our deepest intentions. In the silence of this *night of faith* we return to simplicity and sincerity of heart. We learn *recollection* which consists in listening for God's will, in direct and simple attention to *reality*. Recollection is awareness of the unconditional. *Prayer* then means yearning for the simple presence of God, for a personal understanding of his Word, for knowledge of his will and for capacity to hear and obey him. It is thus something much more than uttering petitions for good things external to our deepest concerns.[11]

This is when we allow the presence of the Lord to speak to us about our own needs. This is where we evaluate ourselves and are able to understand purpose and meaning in our lives as the children of the Lord. We may be reminded about something we said, or an inappropriate act. I have been reminded about promises that I made and forgot. I have also felt the need to cleanse my heart. I have felt my own unworthiness and felt humbled by the touch of the Lord's Spirit. It is like turning on a light in a partially lit room. When the light comes on everything becomes visible in the room. When the Spirit of the Lord comes, there is a revealing of areas in our lives that were not noticed prior to His appearance. This can be very revealing, because sometimes we are not aware of our needs.

> When the Spirit of the Lord comes, there is a revealing of areas in our lives that were not noticed prior to His appearance.

When we are meditating on the stories in the Scriptures, there is often identification with the story or person mentioned. The accounts may not be identical, but there are often similarities. This enables us to "bring it closer to home" and apply the Scriptures to our own lives.

By identifying ourselves with God's people—Jesus, the prophets and the great men and women of the Old and New Testaments—we find ourselves adopting their attitudes. We also recognize ourselves in the bad characters of the text—the Pharisees, Pharaoh, the apostles when they were jealous of each other—and find that we want to give up these attitudes.[12]

The greatest benefit has to be that we find ourselves being embraced by the love and compassion of the Lord. Kempis said,

> Love is a great and good thing, and alone makes heavy burdens light and bears in equal balance things pleasing and displeasing. Love bears a heavy burden and does not feel it, and love makes bitter things tasteful and sweet. The noble love of Jesus perfectly imprinted in man's soul makes a man do great things, and stirs him always to desire perfection and to grow more and more in grace and goodness.[13]

It is often overwhelming to feel the love that the Lord Jesus has for me. His grace is still amazing! This, of course, makes me want to love Him in return. As Douglas V. Steere in "The Inner Springs of Prayer" said,

> There can be no complete prayer life that does not return to the point from which we began – the prayer that is a response to the outpouring love and concern with which God lays siege to every soul. When that reply to God is most direct of all, it is called *adoration*. Adoration is *loving back*. For in

the prayer of adoration we love God for himself, for his very being, for his radiant joy."[14]

It is very difficult to describe the feeling of God's embrace. It is humbling, while at the same time it is consoling. The classic passage by the apostle Paul says it best.

Love is patient, love is kind. It does not envy, it does not boast, it is not proud. It is not rude, it is not self-seeking, it is not easily angered, it keeps no record of wrongs. Love does not delight in evil but rejoices with the truth. It always protects, always trusts, always hopes, always perseveres. Love never fails... (1 Corinthians 13:4-8 NIV).

Essential Faith

Lectio Divina encourages faith. Faith is an essential ingredient to pleasing God (Hebrews 11). In *lectio divina* there is an anticipation of receiving something from the Lord. First, you seek his presence. Next you anticipate having the Lord speak to you, either from his Word or in your thoughts. Then we also anticipate receiving direction or an answer to our requests or needs.

In much of our traditional praying, we just present our list of requests. We may mix worship and praise in as well, but often we do not take the time to listen for an answer from the Spirit of the Lord. Listening, as I have said before, can sometimes be very difficult. As I was praying this morning, my mind began to wander. I would find myself thinking about people and other things totally apart from what I was praying. I had to make myself concentrate on the prayers that I was praying. When I have difficulty concentrating or focusing in my prayers, I begin to worship and praise the Lord for all of His goodness to me. This brings his presence and helps me to re-focus my praying.

The Scriptures teach us the importance of having faith. "But without faith it is impossible to please him: for he that cometh to God must believe that he is, and that he is a rewarder of them that diligently seek him" (Hebrews 11:6). *Lectio Divina* is not only man speaking to God but allowing God to speak to man. It doesn't matter what form of prayer we use; if we do not have faith in God when we pray, nothing will happen.

There is nothing sacred about *Lectio Divina*, as it is just a method we use to communicate and fellowship with the Lord. The position of the body does not matter. It is not kneeling, standing, sitting or lying prostrate on the ground that impresses God and attracts His presence. It is the condition of our hearts that the Lord is looking at and responding to.

When the children of Israel sinned against God and fiery serpents were sent among them, those who were bitten by the serpents died. The Lord told Moses to make a serpent of brass and put it upon a pole, and all that were bitten would be healed when they looked on the serpent on the pole. Years later the children of Israel worshipped the brazen serpent on the pole. When Hezekiah became King, he destroyed all forms of idols and broke in pieces the brazen serpent, calling it *Nehushtan*, which means a piece of brass (2 Kings 18:1-4). There is a danger that we as humans want to make "things" sacred, instead of God.

There is much value in the teachings about prayer and its importance. Many books have been written on the subject of prayer, some of which I have read and own. However, there is no substitute for the actual practice of prayer in a person's life. I feel that what we need to do is become more involved in prayer on a daily basis. Prayer is very personal and intimate between an individual and the Lord. What a wonderful privilege we have to communicate with the King of Kings and the Lord of Lords.

Conclusion

I have benefited from the study of *Lectio Divina*. However, putting it into practice has not been easy for me. I have been accustomed to praying in a more traditional style. I have found that being more reflective and taking my time while praying and reading the Word of God is very beneficial. This I have put into practice on many occasions. There have been several times that I know that the Lord has spoken to me from a specific Scripture. Each time it was just what I needed.

For several weeks, during the time of this writing, my brother was ill with a terminal disease. This, of course, was on my mind daily. I was able to spend about ten days with him over our spring break. During that time we were able to share together and to read Scriptures together. As I would pray each day, I continued to feel the comfort of His presence. After I had returned home from Phoenix where he lived, I received word that he had passed away. Even though this was not unexpected, I still felt very sorrowful.

While in prayer, I asked the Lord to give me a Scripture to help me to understand the loss of my brother. When I opened the Bible, I read, "The Lord has done this, and it is marvelous in our eyes. This is the day the Lord has made; let us rejoice and be glad in it" (Psalm 118:23-24). Many other Scriptures came to my mind about eternity and living in heaven. I began to reflect on how much better it was for my brother to be with the Lord and with many of our loved ones who have gone on before us. Although I wept and mourned his passing, I realized that this was not the end.

> **The times that the Lord spoke to me most often were when I was still and listening for His voice.**

In the book *The Divine Conspiracy*, Dallas Willard quoted Dwight Moody, "One day soon you will hear that I am dead. Do not believe it. I will then be alive as never before."[15] When the two guards came to take Dietrich Bonhoeffer to the gallows, he briefly took a friend aside to say, "This is the end, but for me it is the beginning of life."[16]

As I reflect over my life, I can remember that the times that the Lord spoke to me most often were when I was still and listening for His voice. When I was a young man in my early twenties, my father gave me some excellent advice. His words were, "Son, you need to be a better listener." I did not realize at the time just how valuable these words were to become. I desire still to become a better listener. I am listening to hear from the Lord and to feel His wonderful presence.

[1] *"Take a look at your Prayer Life, Lectio Divina"* (Saginaw, Michigan) online, available from http://www.saginaw.org/prayer_lectio.htm.
[2] Luke Dysinger, *Accepting the Embrace of God: The Ancient Art of Lectio Divina*, online, available from http://www.valyermo.com/ld-art.html.
[3] Michel de Verteuil, *Lectio Divina – Sacred Reading, A Method of Bible Reflection;* online; available from http://www.clubi.ie/shalom/lectio/method.html.
[4] Dysinger.
[5] Thomas Keating, *The Classical Monastic Practice of Lectio Divina,* online, available from http://www.centeringprayer.com/lectio.htm.
[6] Jeanne Guyon, *Experiencing the Depths of Jesus Christ* (Sargent, GA: SeedSowers Christian Books Publishing, 1975), 96.
[7] Thomas R. Kelly, *A Testament of Devotion* (San Francisco: Harper Collins, 1992), 4.
[8] Evelyn Underhill, "What do we mean by Prayer?", in *Devotional Classics*, eds. Richard J. Foster and James Bryan Smith (San Francisco: Harper Collins, 1993), 112.
[9] Dallas Willard, *The Divine Conspiracy, Rediscovering our Hidden Life in God* (San Francisco: Harper Collins, 1997), 80.
[10] Thomas à Kempis, *The Imitation of Christ* (Garden City, NY: Image Books, 1955), 75.
[11] Thomas Merton, *Contemplative Prayer* (Garden City, NY: Image Books, 1971), 67.
[12] Verteuil.
[13] Kempis, 110.
[14] Douglas V. Steere, "The Inner Springs of Prayer," in *Devotional Classics,* eds. Richard J. Foster and James Bryan Smith (San Francisco: Harper Collins, 1993), 90-91.
[15] Willard, 87, quoting Dwight Moody.
[16] Willard, 87, quoting Dietrich Bonhoeffer.

Faculty Resources

Books by Daniel L. Segraves

You Can Understand the Bible	$15.00
Proverbs: Ancient Wisdom for Today's World	12.00
Romans: Living By Faith	15.00
Themes From a Letter to Rome	11.00
Hebrews: Better Things, Volume 1	11.00
Hebrews, Better Things, Volume 2	11.00
James: Faith at Work	10.00
1 Peter: Standing Fast in the Grace of God	12.00
2 Peter and Jude	12.00
Hair Length in the Bible	7.00
The Messiah's Name: JESUS, not Yahshua	7.00
God in Flesh: Was Jesus' Flesh Heavenly or Earthly?	9.00

Book by Daniel & Judy Segraves

Marriage: Back to Bible Basics $11.00

Books by Judy Segraves

The Marriage-Go-Round $11.00
Been There Done That 10.00
65 Short Stories: A Collection for Enjoyment, 14.00
Encouragement, and Enrichment

Books by Gayla M. Baughman

Christian Social Graces: $16.00
A Guide for the Pentecostal Woman
Companion Workbook: for Christian Social Graces 13.00
To Have and To Hold: Wedding Planner 12.50

Books by Terry R. Baughman

Grace is a Pentecostal Message $11.00
Mysteries of the Kingdom: Gentile Inclusion in the 15.00
Kingdom of Heaven as revealed in the Parables of Mt. 13
Let's Go! Life & Ministry of Mark Baughman 11.00
Preach It! Selected Sermons of Mark Baughman 12.00

Faculty Resources

Books by Laura Payne

Creative Composition: A guide to writing Gospel Songs	$16.00
Applied Piano Book 1	12.00
(a chord method book using Roman Numerals – progresses through sevenths)	
Applied Piano Book 2	12.00
(a continuation of Book 1, using both Roman Numerals and letter names)	

Music by Laura Payne and the Christian Life College choir

Rain (1998) CD	$15.00
Rain Cassette	10.00
Rain Soundtrack	50.00
Rain Choral Packet	15.00
1in U (2000) CD	15.00
1in U Cassette	10.00
1in U Soundtrack	50.00
1in U Choral Packet	15.00
Heart of Worship (2001) CD	15.00
Heart of Worship Cassette	10.00
Heart of Worship Soundtrack	50.00
Heart of Worship Choral Packet	15.00
Surrendered in Worship (2002) CD	15.00
Surrendered in Worship Cassette	10.00
Surrendered in Worship Choral Packet	15.00

Christian Life College

To order these faculty resources indicate number of each title desired, add sales tax (7.75%), and 15% shipping & handling charges (20% Canadian/30% Foreign)

Make Checks payable and mail to:

Christian Life College Bookstore
9023 West Lane • Stockton, CA 95210
Bookstore: 209.476.7897
College office: 209.476.7840
Fax: 209.476.7868
Website: www.clc.edu

Ship to: (Please Print)

Name		
Address		
City	St	Zip
Phone		
Email		